W9-DJE-247

COPING THROUGH ASSERTIVENESS

by Rhoda McFarland

THE ROSEN PUBLISHING GROUP, INC.

NEW YORK

Published in 1986 by The Rosen Publishing Group, Inc.
29 East 21st Street, New York City, New York 10010

First Edition
Copyright 1986 by Rhoda McFarland

Library of Congress Cataloging-in-Publication Data

McFarland, Rhoda.
    Coping through assertiveness.

    Includes index.
    1. Assertiveness (Psychology)   I. Title.
BF575.A85M36   1986   158′.1   86-599
ISBN 0-8239-0680-9

Manufactured in the United States of America

About the Author

Rhoda McFarland is a teacher who has had experience teaching all grades kindergarten through twelfth grade. At the junior and senior high levels she has taught a variety of academic subjects and has been a band and choir director as well. She is still active as a musician and plays bass clarinet in the Sacramento Valley Symphonic Band, a community organization of non-professional musicians.

Ms. McFarland has worked with troubled young people and their parents as a teacher and certified alcoholism and drug abuse counselor. She is responsible for writing and implementing the first educational program in the central California area for students making the transition from drug/alcohol treatment programs back into the regular school system. Because of her extensive training and background in the field of chemical dependency, she is sought as a consultant by treatment facilities, parent groups, and educational programs. She is highly respected in her community for her talents and dedication in helping troubled families.

Parents have profited from Ms. McFarland's ability to work with difficult young people by taking workshops from her on practical techniques for dealing with acting-out behavior. Teaching parents to cope assertively is a major part of the workshops. A natural step from teaching assertiveness for parents was taking those same techniques and developing them for young people.

iii

Contents

CHAPTER I

How You Learned to Cope with Problems

Are you tired of being hassled by unreasonable parents? Do teachers frustrate and irritate you? Why is it that every time you say something to adults they get on your case? Even friends are hard to get along with sometimes; you never know when they are going to get mad at some little thing that is no big deal. And what about the people who get their feelings hurt and you do not even know why? Sometimes it is hard to know what to do or what to say. Why is that?

You have never been taught how to deal with people assertively. Everything you know and do in your relationships with people, you learned from others. When you were a baby you learned about behavior from the people in your life. No one said, "This is what you say, and this is what you do in this situation." You watched what adults did and listened to what they said. As you grew, you tried out what you saw and heard. If what you did was okay with the people around you, good things came down. If they did not like what you said and did, bad things came down. So you learned by trial and error, by guess and by golly. As a result, much of your behavior today is automatic.

What you learned were ways of behaving that were successful for you and the people in your life. The fact that the behavior patterns were successful (achieved what was wanted or needed) does not mean that they were the most beneficial or most effective ways to behave. In fact, they could be very destructive and cause you problems with other people.

Should you blame your parents for teaching you behavior patterns that are causing you problems? Before you do, consider that they were doing the best they could to get along the only way they knew how. Their behavior was automatic, too. They were taught the same way you were and just passed it right along to you.

When you were old enough, you went to school, where new influences came into your life. Teachers told you things about your behavior—what was acceptable, and what was not. They showed you adult behavior that you may not have experienced before. You became involved with friends and their parents. You watched

1

and listened to the way they handled their problems and learned more about relating to others. You may have become involved in church activities, where you watched and listened. After-school activities in Brownies or Boy Scouts or sports meant that you had more people to watch and to listen to. All of these people influenced you and your interaction with others. Sometimes you were scolded and punished, and you did not know why. Perhaps, if you asked, you were told, "You know what you did!" Not much help, was it?

As you grew, you may have noticed more and more that you were trying to guess what would be allowed and what would make people upset. Perhaps you never tried to guess and went ripping along wondering why people were on your case all the time. At any rate, you probably had very little help in learning to deal with others directly and honestly. It is likely that you watched scenes like this one between Dad, who is an hour late, and Mom, who spent the entire afternoon cooking a special dinner.

MOM: Well, it's about time you got home. Dinner is ruined.
DAD: Oh, I'm sorry, honey. I stopped to get the oil changed, and it took longer than I expected.
MOM: You could have called.
DAD: I didn't think I'd be very late.

Mom says nothing more and puts dinner on the table. She hardly speaks during the meal, but Dad does not notice because he and Son are discussing the football game that will be on TV in a few minutes. After dinner Dad and Son watch the game.

Mom is still angry because Dad was late and is even more angry because he did not notice the special dinner she had spent so much time preparing; and, even worse, he did not even notice that she was upset. She finishes cleaning the kitchen, goes into the living room where Dad and Son are watching TV, and begins picking up magazines and papers and slamming them on the table. Dad notices that Mom seems upset.

DAD: What's wrong, honey?
MOM: Nothing. (Walks out of the room.)
DAD: (To Son.) Do you know what she's mad about?
SON: I don't have a clue, Dad; she was like that when I sat down at the dinner table.

Mom is playing the Great American Game of "Guess what I'm feeling." Dad and Son are not very good guessers tonight. It does not look as if Mom is going to get the attention and smoothing of ruffled feathers that she is looking for. She is just going to feel more and more unappreciated, and there may be an argument later because Dad is going to be irritated by the way she is treating him.

What is Son learning about getting along with people? Women get bent out of shape for no reason at all and expect you to know why. Men are treated coldly when they cannot guess why women are upset, and it usually takes an argument before women will tell what is bothering them. The best thing to do when women get bent out of shape is to stay out of the way until the whole thing blows over.

Another Great American Game is "Guess what I really mean." Here is how that game goes:

Mr. Uncleary asked Cuebert and Bentley to help him with an all-day project. He took them to a pizza place for lunch. Seeing video games in the rear, the boys quickly ate lunch and began playing the games. Mr. Uncleary was ready to go back to work, so he went to the boys and said, "Do you want to walk back?"

Cuebert said, "Sure, that's cool," and continued playing as Mr. Uncleary walked out. A few minutes later Mr. Uncleary came back inside and told the boys to quit being wise guys and come on before they were late. Cuebert and Bentley were confused because they were planning to walk back when the game was over. Mr. Uncleary was angry because they had not stopped playing when he asked them if they wanted to walk. He was being sarcastic and thought they knew he meant for them to leave right then. They thought he was seriously telling them they could walk back. Bentley and Cuebert were justifiably annoyed with Mr. Uncleary for not saying what he wanted in the first place. Later they said they would never help him again. Mr. Uncleary said he would never ask them to go with him again. Here was a case of hard feelings on both sides because someone was playing "Guess what I really mean" and the other players guessed wrong.

A third Great American Game is "If I do this, maybe she'll do that." This game is usually played when you do not want to ask someone to do or say something because you are afraid she will say no or think you are silly, so you try to manipulate things so that she will offer to do or say what you want. If it sounds complicated, it certainly is just that. It does not always work, but watch how the game is played.

FRANNY FISHER: I can't get my hair right.
KAY KIND: It looks great.
FRANNY FISHER: Oh, it does not. It looks awful.
KAY KIND: Really, Franny, it looks fine.

Franny is fishing for a *big* compliment, and this can go on until Kay says what Franny wants or until Kay refuses to play any longer and agrees with Franny and makes things really bad!
Vicky Victim plays the game this way:

VICKY VICTIM: I sure would like to go to the game Friday, but I don't have a ride.
PATSY PUSHOVER: (Not wanting to take Vicky, but feeling trapped.) Uh . . . Oh, I guess you could ride with me.

The players in the games never feel good about what is happening. Sometimes one player gets what she wants, but seldom do both participants have their needs met. There are frequently hurt or resentful feelings, and it all comes about because people are not dealing with each other with assertiveness.

Why Do You Need to Be Assertive?

In the Great American Games the players are always focused on the other players. Mom wanted Dad to behave in a particular way; Franny Fisher wanted Kay Kind to say the right thing; Vicky Victim wanted someone to give her a ride without her asking for one; Dad felt guilty and became irritated because of the way Mom was behaving; Kay Kind felt uncomfortable because Franny was fishing for a compliment, and no matter what Kay said it was not right; and poor Patsy Pushover got stuck with Vicky, who was no fun to be around at all. They were all feeling unhappy with their situation and had given responsibility for their feelings to other people. Their sense of happiness and well-being depended on others. Not one person was expressing how he or she honestly felt about what was happening. They all gave away their right to be responsible for their own feelings. The quality of their lives and their relationships depended on other people. They all thought they were victims of circumstance and blamed someone else for their feelings of unhappiness. No wonder they were caught in the Great American Games: They were looking in the wrong place for good relationships with others.

The quality of *your* relationships depends upon *you*. If you wait for others to do something about their relationship with you, you are in for a long wait. Only one person can do anything about the quality of your relationships, and that is you! It is time to take charge and accept responsibility for your life and for what goes on in it.

Assertiveness is a means of taking control of yourself and expressing your feelings in appropriate ways. It is a way to improve your relationships with others by taking responsibility for your wants, needs, and feelings and by making them known to others in ways that protect your rights and respect theirs. It keeps the focus on you and what you are doing so that you do not get into the Great American Game.

Handling situations with assertiveness means treating others with dignity and respect; but, more important, treating yourself with dignity and respect. In every encounter you have, you are either being good to yourself or hurting yourself, being respectful to yourself or disrespectful, behaving with dignity or without dignity. How you feel about yourself after you have expressed your feelings to someone is vitally important to your self-esteem. If you feel good about how you handled things, your self-esteem will go up. You will like yourself. When you get your needs met assertively through appropriate behavior, you will feel good and those around you will feel good. No one will have to play guessing games and take chances on guessing wrong.

It is obvious that playing the Great American Guessing Games is not the way to achieve comfortable relationships with people. If you want to improve relationships with older people, younger people, or people your own age, you need a positive, direct way of dealing with others. You need to replace the games with behavior that expresses your wants and needs in appropriate ways. Assertiveness is your key to happier relationships with others.

CHAPTER II

Coping Choices

Suzie Scholar worked really hard on her algebra homework. Tracy Carbon did not do his homework. He never does, and today he wants to copy Suzie's. He is not a friend of Suzie's, but he sits near her in class and knows she gets good grades. What should Suzie do? How would you handle the situation, and how would that affect the other person involved? Can you handle the situation in such a way that you will feel good about yourself no matter what happens? That is what assertiveness is all about. It is a way of expressing your true feelings honestly and directly in an appropriate way without infringing on the rights of others.

In handling the situation with Tracy, Suzie needs first to decide what she is feeling. She may be thinking, "I don't want to let him copy my work. I worked hard and it isn't fair for him to get credit for what I do. I don't even know him. Why should I give him my work?" Suzie's true feeling is that she does not want to let Tracy copy her work, but what will he think if she says no? Will he put her down and make nasty comments about her to other people? Will he make fun of her to make her look bad? That would be awful—or would it? Who is running her life, Suzie or Tracy? She will feel resentful if she is nonassertive and lets Tracy copy her work, and Tracy will be running her life. If she is in charge of her life, she will be assertive and say, "I worked really hard on this. I'm not going to let anyone copy my work." A third choice would be an aggressive response: "No way, man, do your own work and don't try to cheat off mine!"

In any situation where there is a conflict of interest, you have three coping choices: assertive, nonassertive (passive), and aggressive. Do not confuse assertive with aggressive. The purpose of an assertive response is to express your feelings and protect your rights without harming others or infringing on their rights. When you are assertive, you protect the rights of others as well as your own. An aggressive response expresses your rights and feelings without regard for the rights of others. An aggressive response dominates and overpowers. It is meant to put others down. The typical attitude of an aggressive person is, "Nobody does that to me and gets away with it." Passive people deny and neglect their own feelings, do not communicate directly and honestly, and allow others to infringe on their rights.

Not knowing their own feelings is a major problem for people who want to become assertive. When you disregard your own feelings and concentrate on how other people are feeling or may be feeling, you lose your own feelings. You do not know how you truly feel. You may decide how you think you "should" feel, but that denies how you really feel. Since assertiveness requires that you express your true feelings honestly and directly, you have no chance of being assertive until you get in touch with your feelings.

Using the episode with Tracy Carbon, what might Suzie feel about Tracy? She probably feels very uncomfortable to have been put in such a position. She might feel angry because Tracy is trying to take advantage of her. She could feel trapped because she feels pressure from Tracy to do something she doesn't want to do. She may feel resentful that someone she does not know well would make such a demand of her. She could feel afraid of how Tracy will react if she says no. She may feel guilty because she feels she "should" help people but does not want to "help" Tracy.

Suzie's feelings tell her that she does not want to let Tracy copy her homework. The kind of response Suzie gives him will depend on what kind of person she is and how important the opinion of others is to her. A natural response to what Suzie is feeling is an aggressive, "No way, man, go cheat off someone else!" However, it is inappropriate because it would be a put-down calling him a cheater (even if he is one), and it does not treat him with dignity and respect. Suzie needs to translate her negative feelings into a dignified response that says no in a way that does not put Tracy down and leaves Suzie feeling good about herself. The assertive response, "I worked really hard on this, and I'm not letting anybody copy my work," says all she needs to say. It does not put Tracy down, and it says no gracefully but with finality.

If Suzie is very concerned about what Tracy will think of her if she says no and of what others will think of her if Tracy tells them she would not let him copy her homework, unwarranted guilt and fear will cause her to deny the feelings that tell her to say no to Tracy. She will be passive and allow Tracy to copy. She will not have treated herself with dignity and respect, she will feel resentful toward Tracy, and she will not like herself.

How People Become Aggressive or Passive

Passive and aggressive behavior do not require that you analyze your true feelings and choose your responses. They are automatic and come to you without thought. Aggressive people have angry feelings that cover up almost all of their other feelings. To them it is not okay to feel hurt or afraid. If they are frightened, they cover it up with anger. Passive people, on the other hand, cover up their angry feelings with hurt or even nothingness. To them, it is okay to feel nothing or to feel hurt.

Boys are taught that it is not manly to be afraid, to cry, to let people know their feelings are hurt. They are supposed to "take it like a man." In our society, to be a man means not to show your feelings, but you can get angry. "Real men" get angry and break things or even hit people. They tell other people where to get off and do it in a loud, snarly voice so the other person will be afraid and know better than to mess with them. Everything they do is to protect their cover of "strong and manly."

People do not just suddenly tell themselves that it is okay to be angry but not okay to feel afraid, powerless, unsure, tender, soft, or all those other things that to them mean weak. Randy Roarer was taught to disregard his tender feelings. When Randy was little and fell down and hurt himself, his parents said, "Big boys don't cry." When Randy's Uncle Al was killed in an automobile accident, his father took it like a man, did not shed a tear or miss a day's work other than the day of the funeral even though he and Al were as close as brothers could be. Randy felt really bad because Uncle Al was his favorite uncle, and he would really miss him; but if Dad could get through it okay, so could Randy. Dad was pretty grouchy for a while, but you could not blame him. It was rough on him, and he had every right to be short-tempered.

When Randy was in sixth grade, the teacher did not like him very much. Randy was not sure why, but Mr. Dour would say things in front of the class that were humiliating to Randy. Randy was confused and hurt and felt like crying. He did not like to feel that way. It made him feel small and like a baby. He wanted to feel big and like a man, and he began to get angry with Mr. Dour. Randy decided that he would get even with Mr. Dour, and he began to do things to make Mr. Dour angry. When Mr. Dour shouted and raged, Randy would just look at him with no expression on his face. From that time on, no teacher ever got the best of Randy.

As Randy grew up, he increasingly denied any feelings he considered weak. He could just pretend he did not care and was ususally pretty easy to get along with, but if anyone did anything that Randy did not like, he let them know about it loud and clear. He did not take anything from anybody.

Inside Randy all of his tender, gentle feelings were trapped. He covered them all up with anger because he was no sissy; he was a man. Now Randy does not know what his feelings are because he has not allowed himself to feel them for so long.

Boys are not the only ones who cover their feelings with anger. Jeanette and Lena were best friends who cared a great deal for each other. One day at school, Jeanette was feeling down, and Lena stopped by her locker to talk for a minute.

LENA: What are you doing after school today?
JEANETTE: (Snapping.) Nothing. I want to be alone.
LENA: Is something wrong?
JEANETTE: (Snarling.) No, nothing's wrong, just leave me alone.
LENA: I didn't mean to make you mad.
JEANETTE: (Shouting.) Will you just buzz off and leave me alone?
LENA: (Shouting.) If you're gonna be such a witch, I'll be glad to leave you alone!

Later, talking over the situation with a counselor, Jeanette said that she was feeling upset about something that had happened at home. She had lashed out at the first person who came along. Lena had been so shocked and hurt at the way Jeanette treated her that her anger came out, also. Both girls were hiding their true feelings behind their anger. They had learned to cover their tender, gentle feelings, too. They did not want to be hurt, so they got angry and aggressive.

When Patsy Pushover was a little girl and was angry and shouted, "I hate you!" to her brother, her mother said, "That's not nice. You shouldn't hate your brother. You tell him you're sorry." When Patsy came into the room with an angry look on her face, her father said, "You go right back through that door, young lady, and come into this room with a smile on your face."

Patsy was never allowed to show anger, so she covers it up with a smile. She heard over and over again, "Nice girls don't hate their brothers. Nice girls don't stomp around the house. Nice girls don't

act pushy. Nice girls don't shout. Nice girls don't get angry."
Patsy's life was a long list of "Nice girls don't. . . ." She tried very
hard to please her parents and be nice. She smiled and was always
pleasant. She cried sometimes, too, especially when people
treated her badly. When other children were cruel to her and teased
her, she would run home crying. Her mother would wipe away her
tears and tell her how naughty the other children were and what a
nice girl she was.

As Patsy grew up, she was always nice to people. Whenever
anyone asked a favor, Patsy helped out. She was always on the
dance clean-up committees. She would help teachers after school,
even though she had planned to go to a friend's and watch videos.
Patsy would lend her tapes to friends who would keep them for
weeks, and Patsy never complained. She was nice.

Patsy was always concerned about how other people felt. She
wanted them to like her. She never thought of how she was
feeling, whether or not she was happy. Actually, Patsy was not
very happy, but she did not know that because she had lost touch
with her true feelings. She did not like being taken advantage of,
but she knew she should be nice to other people and should not
feel angry. As long as she was being nice and people liked her, she
thought she should be happy.

How Your Feelings Were Lost

As you have been growing up, just like Patsy and Randy people
have been telling you which of your feelings are acceptable. They
have not been listening when you tell them how you feel, because
when you do tell them, they say, "You shouldn't feel that way," or
"I know how you *really* feel." When people do that, they are
telling you that your feelings do not count, that you are not feeling
"right" about things. Of course, the right way is the way they feel
or think they would feel under the same circumstances. The sad
thing about it is that you allow them to influence you. You allow
them to convince you of how you "should" feel. When you let
people "should" on you, you judge your feelings as bad. You tell
yourself that your true feelings do not count, and you end up piling
"should" all over yourself.

When you get into a pile of "should," your feelings are all
covered up. Instead of asking yourself, "What am I feeling?" you
ask yourself, "What should I be feeling?" If you feel angry, you tell
yourself, "I shouldn't be mad about such a little thing." When you

feel hurt from a put-down, you say, "I shouldn't let that bother me; she was just kidding," or "He can't say that to me. I should get him back." When someone takes advantage of you and you feel insulted, you dismiss it with, "I shouldn't be upset. He didn't mean to be rude," or "How dare he say such a thing to me. I should tell him off for that!" You also get into all the "should's" that have to do with what you "should" do when you do not want to and where you "should" go when you would rather not. No wonder you lose your feelings with all that "should" piled on!

How to Find Your Feelings

You can claim your feelings again if you stop judging your feelings. Stop telling yourself, "I shouldn't feel this way," or "It's bad to feel this way." Simply say, "I feel angry; I feel sad; I feel guilty; I feel excited; I feel embarrassed; I feel happy; I feel insulted; I feel ashamed; I feel anxious; I feel lonely." Whatever you feel, acknowledge the feeling and accept it. It is okay to feel. All those feelings you may have judged as bad are *not* bad. All those feelings you may think are good are *not* good. Feelings are neither good nor bad, they just are. What you *do* about them may be good or bad. It is sometimes difficult to express feelings appropriately. The key to appropriate expression of feelings is assertiveness.

Expressing Feelings with Assertiveness, Aggressiveness, or Passiveness

You always have three choices for expressing your feelings in any situation: assertiveness, aggressiveness, or passiveness. To be assertive is to express your feelings honestly, directly, and appropriately in a way that does not violate the rights of others. To be aggressive is to express yourself without regard for the rights of others with the purpose of dominating and overpowering. To be passive is to not communicate directly and honestly, denying or neglecting your own feelings, ignoring your own rights, and allowing others to infringe on them.

Here are some situations to demonstrate the three options for expressing feelings:

Aggressive

Kevin Kombat wants to cut to the front of Randy Roarer in the lunch line.

KEVIN: Let me get in front of you.
RANDY: Hey, man, no cuts.
KEVIN: Hey, dude, I just wanna buy a milkshake. No big deal.
RANDY: Yeah, well go cut in front of somebody else; nobody cuts in front of me.

(To protect his own rights, Randy chooses to overpower and dominate Kevin and is willing to defend his rights without regard for Kevin's rights. Randy thinks Kevin does not deserve to have his rights protected or to be treated respectfully.)

Passive

Kevin Kombat wants to cut in front of Patrick Pushover.

KEVIN: Let me cut in front of you.
PATRICK: Uh ... Ah ... well ...
KEVIN: I just wanna buy a milkshake. No big deal.
PATRICK: Well, if that's all you're gonna buy ...

(Patrick does not want Kevin to think that he is selfish, and he is just a little afraid of what Kevin might do if he does not let him in line. Patrick ignores his own rights and feelings in favor of Kevin's; he does not treat himself with dignity and respect.)

Assertive

Kevin Kombat wants to cut in front of Mitchell Moderate.

KEVIN: Let me in front of you.
MITCHELL: I've been waiting ten minutes and I don't want to give cuts.
KEVIN: I just wanna buy a milkshake. No big deal.
MITCHELL: I've been waiting. I don't want to give cuts.
KEVIN: Well, I'll cut somewhere else, man.

(Mitchell does not allow Kevin to infringe on his rights, but he does not put Kevin down. He treats Kevin with dignity and respect and does the same for himself.)

Aggressive

After P.E., Phyllis Friendly wants to borrow a brush from Ruby Roarer.

PHYLLIS: Can I borrow your brush?
RUBY: No way! You could have cooties or something. Nobody uses my brush but me.

(Ruby's aggressive manner is a put-down to Phyllis and shows her no respect.)

Passive

After P.E., Phyllis Friendly wants to borrow a brush from Patsy Pushover.

PHYLLIS: Can I borrow your brush?
PATSY: Well, uh, I'm going to use it now.
PHYLLIS: Oh, I'll wait until you're done. I don't mind.
PATSY: Uh...okay...

(Patsy tries to avoid saying no to Phyllis even though she wants to; she is caught and neglects her own rights.)

Assertive

After P.E., Phyllis Friendly asks to borrow a brush from Melody Moderate.

PHYLLIS: Can I borrow your brush?
MELODY: I don't lend my brush.
PHYLLIS: I just need it for a minute.
MELODY: I don't lend my brush to anyone.

(Melody's assertive statement does not put Phyllis down, nor does it invite her to continue the discussion further. Melody has taken care of her own rights without infringing on Phyllis's.)

Getting Mom to stop smoking is the goal:

Aggressive

RANDY: Why don't you quit smoking? You're always telling me to eat right and all that stuff and you smoke at least two packs a day.
MOM: I'm an adult, and if I want to smoke, that's my business.

RANDY: I have to live in your second-hand smoke, and Mr. Scientific says that second-hand smoke is as bad as if I smoked myself. Besides, the ashtrays are nasty.
MOM: You don't have to clean them, so stop complaining.

(This argument can go on indefinitely and can go in a variety of directions. Randy has put his mother on the defensive, and she is not going to discuss the matter reasonably.)

Passive

PATSY: Mom, may I open the window?
MOM: It's not too warm in here, Patsy, we don't need the window open.
PATSY: Well, uh ... uh ... the cigarette smoke is real bad.
MOM: Oh, I didn't notice, honey. I guess I'm used to its being smoky in here.
PATSY: Well, uh ... you do smoke an awful lot.
MOM: Yeah, I keep telling myself I'm going to cut down, but I never do.
PATSY: That would probably be a good idea, Mom.
MOM: You're probably right, Patsy.

(Patsy and her mother could go on talking for an hour and Patsy would never get around to directly asking her to quit smoking.)

Assertive

MELODY: Mom, I'm really concerned about your smoking.
MOM: Oh, you're going to start in on that again, are you?
MELODY: Not exactly, Mom. I just want you to know that I love you a lot, and I don't want anything to happen to you. I'm worried that since you smoke so much you might get cancer or heart disease.
MOM: I appreciate your concern, honey, but you don't need to worry about me.
MELODY: I do, though, Mom, and I just wanted you to know how I feel. I hope you'll think about quitting.

(Melody has expressed her feelings in a caring and respectful way. Her mother won't stop smoking, at least not today; but Melody has told her mother how she feels in an appropriate way and can feel good about the conversation.)

How Aggressiveness Makes You a Loser

There is a saying, "What goes around, comes around." Aggressive people may get their way, but it is important to look at what comes around to them. The Randy and Ruby Roarers always seem to be defending themselves. It seems that people are forever getting into Randy's space and giving him grief. Behavior that would get little reaction from others gets major reaction from Randy. He makes a big deal power play out of everything. Nobody is going to put anything over on him. Because of his attitude, nobody can get close to Randy. He is so defensive that people have to tiptoe around him. He is like an octopus with all eight tentacles waving around waiting for someone to step on them. When you try to step over one, another one whips around under your foot, and there you are, treading on Randy no matter how hard you try to avoid it. After a while, people get tired of trying to avoid stepping on Randy and simply avoid him altogether. They leave him alone, and he ends up lonely and frustrated. Randy needs to know that when you do not let people get close, they stay away.

Randy and Ruby always seem to be fighting with others. It seems arguments come looking for Ruby. She says, "I don't go looking for trouble, but when somebody pushes me, I push back." Being like an octopus, Ruby has her feelers out for offenses all the time. She will feel offended whether or not offense was meant. Soon the only people who go around Ruby are the aggressive people who are spoiling for a fight, too. What goes around, comes around.

How does Ruby feel? She feels angry, powerful, forceful, strong, self-righteous, and sometimes guilty about the way she has treated someone, lonely because people do not like her, confused because others do not understand her, and maybe even a little afraid that someone might discover that under that roaring and aggressiveness is someone who is afraid that other people might hurt her.

Randy and Ruby are not winners. Their losses are great. They have lost the positive regard and respect of people, who are afraid of being put down and dominated and feel they must give Randy and Ruby plenty of space. Inside, Randy and Ruby do not feel good about themselves, or they would not be so defensive. They do not even feel good about the way they think they have to treat people. They have lost their true feelings because they cover tender, gentle, soft feelings with anger. Their greatest loss of all is their loss of dignity and self-respect.

How Passiveness Makes You a Loser

Poor, pitiful Patsy and Patrick Pushover seldom have their needs met while allowing other people to take advantage of them. They are easy to identify by the footprints on their faces where people have walked all over them. However, there are lots of Patricks and Patsys who look like winners.

Since he is so nice and so helpful, Patrick is always asked to be on committees and to be a part of school activities. He is very capable and does his own job and someone else's, if necessary. He gets good grades, is involved in sports and music, and is active in church activities. At home, Patrick is responsible and dependable. Everyone thinks he is wonderful, except Patrick. Patrick cannot say no. He cannot tell teachers that he does not want any more responsibility. He cannot tell his mother that watching his little brother and sister two or three times a week makes him angry. He cannot tell friends that he does not want to help them with their geometry when they phone. Patrick is doing everything for everybody but himself. His feelings are all bottled up inside, and he has ignored them for so long that he has lost them.

Most people would not call Patsy a loser. They probably would not call her anything, because they would not notice her. If they did, they might say, "Oh, yeah, she was in my English class. Real quiet." Patsy is terribly alone. She is afraid to speak up, to let people know she is alive. People just walk past her and disregard her. She seems to be a nonperson. She will agree to almost anything. Patsy does not do much; it seems so hard to get going. She never talks back or is disagreeable at home, but she never gets things done. If she starts to clean her room, something happens and it does not get done. Her parents sometimes lose patience with her, but they cannot be too angry because Patsy cries and tells them she is trying hard.

At school Patsy has problems, too. She does not get all of her work done, but teachers tend to let things slide because Patsy is no problem in class. She just seems to be a little slow. She is often late to class, but she can slip in without being seen if the teacher is talking to a student or if any activity is going on.

Patsy always looks a little lost, and that is no surprise because she is. Other people seem to know how to deal with the world, but

Patsy has no idea. She does not try to figure things out, because people always tell her how she should feel and what she should do. When she does have a feeling about something, she is usually told that she shouldn't feel that way, so Patsy does not trust her feelings and has learned to ignore them.

Whether they are taken advantage of because they allow others to walk on them or because they are so nice, or disregarded because they fade into the wallpaper, the Pushovers are losers. They neglect and ignore their own feelings and allow others to infringe on their rights. Pushovers have deep resentments toward people who treat them badly but cannot express those resentments directly. They do not openly oppose anyone, but they get even in passive ways. You can complain and nag all you want, but Patsy will not be on time. She always has a good excuse, but she is always late. You may not be the one who treats Patsy badly, but her aggressive behavior, though passive, is subconscious and directs everything she does.

Other ways that Patsy and Patrick get even are by not finishing what they start, by not doing things, by forgetting, by accidentally breaking dishes while washing or drying them, by never making a decision, by leaving tools, clothes, dishes, books, or food scraps lying around. They find all kinds of ways to get even without being openly aggressive. Such sneaky tactics are hardly fair. Other people do not recognize them as aggression, and they certainly are frustrating: The indecisiveness sends some people into orbit.

Patrick and Patsy look like victims most of the time. They certainly do not receive dignity and respect from other people. While they are getting even with others, they are not treating others or themselves with dignity and respect. They never feel really good about themselves. Passiveness always equals loser.

How Assertiveness Makes You a Winner

The greatest loss through aggressiveness and passiveness is the loss of your personal dignity and self-respect, and that is what you maintain and enhance with assertiveness. So often your concern is that others, especially adults, do not treat you with respect. YOU DO NOT NEED RESPECT FROM OTHERS BEFORE YOU CAN BE RESPECTFUL TO YOURSELF. It is your responsibility to treat yourself with dignity and respect. Deep inside yourself, how *you* feel about *you* after an encounter with someone else is the most important thing to come out of the exchange.

Melody and Mitchell Moderate did not put anyone down, and they were not interested in overpowering anyone. They expressed their feelings and protected their rights without violating the rights of others. They treated others with dignity and respect even when others had not treated them respectfully. Melody and Mitchell may not always get their way or achieve their goals, but they will always feel good about themselves. They will know that they have expressed themselves honestly, directly, and appropriately. Their self-esteem will be enhanced and their sense of power and self-confidence will grow. As assertiveness is practiced and becomes more and more a part of their coping with situations, Melody and Mitchell will gain respect from others. Being assertive will make them winners.

CHAPTER III

When Coping through Assertiveness Is Difficult

Fred Friendly is one of the most popular boys in school. He is a good athlete and plays on the soccer and baseball teams. Academically in the top quarter of the class, Fred has few problems with schoolwork, and his teachers like him. Both boys and girls enjoy his company because he is easygoing and has a good sense of humor. Girls he hardly knows call him and invite him to dances. Since he did not have a steady girlfriend, Fred went to the homecoming dance, the Christmas dance, and the junior prom with three different girls, all of whom had asked him to take them. Fred really did not want to go with any of them, but he did not know how to say no when they asked him.

Oscar Ordinary is working for the summer at Big Sky Dude Ranch. He feels lucky to have the job; one hundred people applied for three openings, and he was one of the chosen three. Just being around the horses and the cowboys is exciting for Oscar, and he does not mind the hard labor and dirty work that are his to do. At least, he would not mind if it were not for Billy Barks. Because Billy was at Big Sky last year, he thinks he knows everything and is constantly telling Oscar what to do even when Oscar is already doing it. This has been going on since Oscar arrived two weeks ago and is spoiling the entire experience for him. He would like to tell Billy to knock it off, but he does not want to make waves.

Alice Attainer has been chairperson of the student activities committee this year. Five students serve on the committee, but Harold Helper has done most of the real work with Alice. They have become good friends, and Alice will really miss Harold next year, since he is graduating. This being the last meeting of the committee, Alice does not know if she will have another opportunity to tell Harold how much she has appreciated his help all year. The meeting ends, and Alice and Harold are alone. Although

Alice wants very much to thank Harold, she just cannot say how she feels. She says goodbye and walks out feeling very unsatisfied.

When Kevin Kombat came home from the football game, he was really down. The team had won every game this year and had one game standing between them and the regional championships, and they lost it! Kevin could not believe that the receiver had dropped that last pass. Kevin had blocked the only player between him and the goal line, and he dropped the ball! Kevin's dad was telling him not to feel bad and all that garbage. Dad really was trying to be helpful, but Kevin just wanted to be alone. He wished that Dad would just drop it for now.

Since being assertive is the key to being a winner, why is it so difficult for these four people? It is especially difficult for young people to be assertive because you worry about what your peers will think or what the other person involved is thinking and what the reaction will be. Whenever you are caught in such a situation, your first thought is, "I can't say anything. What will s/he think?" If other people are around, you worry about what their reactions will be. You feel everyone's eyes and ears on you. You do not want to do anything that would make people think you are different. Being part of the group is important.

It takes a lot of strength and self-confidence to be assertive. Instead of thinking about others and their reactions, you have to think about how you feel and what you want to do. You have to deal with the problem in a way that does not harm anyone else and makes you feel good about yourself. It is hard to be your own judge instead of trying to figure out how others will judge you and trying to please them. Pleasing yourself is a tall order when peer approval is so important.

Two big worries are that someone might get angry or that you might hurt someone's feelings. Fred did not know how to tell the girls he did not want to go to the dances without hurting their feelings. He gave up his right to spend his time with whom and how he wanted. Oscar did not want to risk Billy's anger. Alice was too self-conscious to thank Harold, and she was afraid he would think she was stupid or something. Kevin thought his dad would be hurt if he said he wanted to be alone. All of these people were focused outside themselves.

When a problem comes up, you must focus on yourself. Though it seems that other people are responsible for creating your problems, the way you deal with those problems determines what your life is like. Look at the four areas that gave so much trouble. Fred could not be assertive when asked to do something he did not want to do. Expressing negative feelings was Oscar's hang-up, while Alice could not express positive feelings. Kevin really had a need to be alone, but he could not tell his dad what he needed.

When People Ask You to Do What You Do Not Want to Do

Some people would say that Fred was very lucky to have so many girls interested in him. Perhaps Fred might have thought so, too, if he had been interested in any of the girls. Actually, he felt resentful toward the girls; all three dates were very expensive, and he did not want to spend so much money on girls who were not special to him. In addition, because Fred did not enjoy himself, the girls did not have a very good time either. In fact, none of them ever called him again.

Saying yes when you want to say no starts out as being a nonassertive, passive response; however, it can end up in aggression. Penny Passive was a good friend of Ima Imposer until she let Ima talk her into doing a special favor. Ima's parents were going out of town on Friday evening and would not return until Sunday evening. Ima was responsible for taking care of her little brother Wiley for the weekend, but she wanted to go out with Tracy Carbon. After Ima had spent weeks plotting and planning to get his attention, Tracy had finally asked her to go to the football game on Saturday afternoon, and Ima just *had* to go. She begged Penny to watch Wiley and promised that she would pick him up right after the game. Ima had already told Tracy that she would go, so Penny felt backed into a corner. She really did not want to take care of Wiley, who was a brat, but she reluctantly agreed to baby-sit.

The day was a total disaster. Wiley was an absolute terror and would not mind Penny at all. The final straw was when he broke her curling iron using it to dig for worms in the backyard. Penny was relieved when the boy next door got home at four to say that their school had won. Ima would be back any minute. By six o'clock Penny was calling Ima's house every five minutes. By nine o'clock she was calling hospitals to check on accident victims. Finally at ten-thirty Ima drove up to the house. The look of ecstasy on her face vanished when Penny came stomping out of the house, dragging a struggling Wiley down the steps. Penny did not give Ima a chance for any explanation. She just blew up, and when the dust cleared, Ima and Wiley were gone and so was the friendship between Penny and Ima.

Neither Fred nor Penny wanted to hurt the feelings of the other people involved by saying no. In both cases, the other people were hurt far worse than an assertively stated "no" would have hurt them.

Saying no is difficult because you think you have to give a good reason for it. When you say no, people always ask why not, and you feel obligated to give them a reason. Since you expect to be asked why not, most of the time you provide the reason without being asked. You have the right to say no, and you do not have to justify and defend your no. If you say yes, does anyone ever ask you why? If a friend asks you to feed her cat while she is on vacation, do you have to give her a reason for saying yes? Of course not! You do not have to give a reason for saying no, either. If it is inconvenient for you to feed her cat, you can just say that.

> YOU: No, I don't want to feed your cat while you're gone. It's really more hassle than I want to take on.
> FRIEND: It's only five minutes to my house.
> YOU: I really don't want to take on that responsibility.
> FRIEND: It will hardly take any time at all.
> YOU: I don't want to feed the cat.

Friend will probably not pursue it any further, but if she does, just say the same thing again. She will soon believe you. She may be frustrated or even angry, but you have done nothing to intrude on her rights. You have simply set your limit. She may become aggressive and try to make you feel guilty for not being a "good" friend. Do not allow her aggression to cause you to give up your right to say no. The resentment that will build inside of you as a result of giving in will do much more damage than your honestly stated and held "no."

Protecting your boundaries is very hard because sometimes you do not realize that people have crossed them. Some examples of boundary crossing are phone calls at times when you do not want to talk, favors asked that you do not want to do, borrowing of money or items you do not want to lend, and expecting you to go places you do not want to go.

When a friend calls and you have something that you need to do, you can handle it with: "I'd really like to talk, but I'm in the middle of something I can't stop now. I'll call you back in an hour when I can talk." If the friend calls about the same time every night, and it is a bad time for you, you can say: "Between six and eight o'clock is a real bad time for me. How about calling back a little after eight and we can talk then?"

For friends who want to borrow things you do not want to lend, you need an assertive statement:

"That's my favorite sweater, and I prefer not to lend it."
"I've had bad luck getting tapes returned, so I don't lend my favorite tapes anymore."

Always remember that you have the right to say no. Fred and Penny could have coped with their problems by assertively saying no.

GIRL 1: I'm going to be in the homecoming parade, and I need an escort. Would you like to go?
FRED: No, but thank you for asking me. I appreciate the invitation.

GIRL 2: It would sure be nice to go to the Christmas Ball. Do you have a date?
FRED: Uh, ...no.
GIRL 2: Neither do I. Maybe we could go together.
FRED: Thanks for suggesting it, but I don't plan to go to the dance.

GIRL 3: This is our junior year and our Junior Prom only comes once. We really should go. Did you ask anybody yet?
FRED: No, I haven't decided if I want to go.
GIRL 3: Well, I don't have a date either.
FRED: I'm not ready to ask anyone yet.

Fred has been kind to the girls, has not put them down in any way, but he has said no. The girls were probably disappointed and may not call him again; but Fred feels good about the way he treated them and feels good about himself.

Ima is a little more difficult to deal with because she really wants to go out with Tracy. When she tells her story to Penny, Ima will be really persuasive.

PENNY: No, I don't want to take care of Wiley.
IMA: I'll only be gone a few hours.
PENNY: I don't want to take care of Wiley.
IMA: Aw, c'mon, be a friend.
PENNY: I'll be your friend, but I won't take care of Wiley.
IMA: What kind of a friend won't do a friend a favor?
PENNY: I won't take care of Wiley.

Penny will have to stand firm because Ima will not give up until she is absolutely sure that she cannot manipulate Penny into taking care of Wiley. Ima will stop taking advantage of Penny when Penny sets her limits and stands firm on her no.

Pressure from others to do things their way or to give them their way puts you in an uncomfortable position. When you feel that discomfort, listen to it and know that you need to treat it with respect. You have the right to say no, and you can say no without infringing on the rights of others while you protect your rights and respect yourself.

When You Want to Express Negative Feelings

Saying that you do not like something, that you feel angry, that you are disappointed, or that you feel negative in any way is very difficult. For most people, the tendency is to hold in negative feelings. George Bach, in his book *The Intimate Enemy*, calls holding negative feelings "gunnysacking." When something happens and you feel uncomfortable about it, you say, "That's no big deal," and you throw the negative feeling into your gunnysack. Something else happens, and you feel a little resentful about it, but you do not want to make an issue of it so you throw it into your gunnysack. Before long, you have such a load that it is too heavy to carry, so you unload it. You dump it out all over everywhere just as Penny did all over Ima. Penny told Ima about every little resentment she had been carrying for months. She said things she had no idea she was capable of saying. Her anger and resentment got the best of her.

As time goes on, Oscar is going to get more and more irritated with Billy. He will fill his gunnysack until it is too full to hold anything more before he expresses his feelings, and then he will do it aggressively and inappropriately. Along with Oscar's present resentment is a withdrawal from Billy. He cannot be friends with Billy because of his gunnysack. Billy is unaware of what he is doing that irritates Oscar, but he knows that Oscar does not like him. Unless Oscar expresses his feelings appropriately, the relationship will be distant and cool.

Levels of Asserting Negative Feelings

If you allow your gunnysack to fill, you will overreact and empty the whole bag in an aggressive way. It is important to remember that *anger should be expressed intentionally in small doses.* If you do not allow the resentments to build, but express them intentionally when each is still small and unimportant, you can avoid filling your gunnysack and expressing them unintentionally in one big dose.

After two weeks of Billy's "helpfulness," Oscar has had it. He shouts, "You don't have to tell me what to do. I know what I'm supposed to do!" Billy is absolutely astounded by the aggression because he was just trying to be helpful. Oscar has fired a cannon at him when all he needed was a peashooter. Oscar came in with what Pamela Butler in *Self-Assertion for Women* calls too high a level of muscle.

When Oscar first realized that Billy was getting on his nerves, he could have used a very low-level muscle. "Billy, I appreciate your help, but I know what I'm supposed to do now, and I would rather not be told." If Billy still told Oscar what to do, Oscar could raise his level of muscle. "I don't want you to tell me what to do." Delivered in a firm tone of voice, this is very straight and to the point. Oscar has not intruded on Billy's dignity, but he is letting Billy know that the continued intrusion is not wanted.

A higher level of muscle would probably not be needed between Oscar and Billy. If it were, it would be time for Oscar to have a talk with the foreman to get job descriptions clarified. If supervising Oscar is not part of Billy's job description, the problem will end with the intervention of the foreman. (High-level muscle.)

Most problems that bring on negative feelings could be handled with low-level muscle. Some low-level ways of expressing negative feelings are:

"I don't agree with you."
"I don't like to be called names."
"I'm angry because we are late for class."
"I'm disappointed that we couldn't go to the movie."
"I feel embarrassed when I'm yelled at."

"I feel put down."

"I feel annoyed when I'm kept waiting."

Sometimes situations call for immediate high-level muscle because of the emotion involved or the seriousness of what is happening. When you put your books down in the library, go to sharpen your pencil, and return to find someone you do not know going through your biology notes, you will not want to deliver a mildly assertive statement. "I resent your going into my things without my permission. Don't you ever do that again!" is an appropriate response for this situation.

How to Know When to Say Something

Whenever you feel that little "zing" of discomfort about what is happening, you can be sure it is your negative feelings trying to talk to you. If you feel resentful toward someone, your feelings need to be expressed. Some clues that let you know your gunnysack is filling are phrases like these: "It's no big deal." "I won't say anything yet." "It's not that bad." "She really didn't mean anything by it." "It's not that important." "He's just trying to be helpful."

The key to keeping your gunnysack empty is expressing your feelings when those little things happen. It *is* important if you toss it into your gunnysack. It *becomes* a big deal if you do not take care of it. She may not have meant anything by it, but it intruded on your rights. A simple assertive statement at those times will take care of your unfinished business. The other person need not do anything or say anything; just stating your feelings will be enough to make you feel better and comfortable about having coped with the situation.

When You Want to Express Positive Feelings

Telling your friend that you think his new shirt is cool is one thing, but telling him that you appreciate the way he listens to you and helps you when you are down is another. Expressing positive feelings can be as hard as expressing negative feelings. Aggressive people take care of negative feelings in inappropriate ways at the expense of others, but they do have their say. Those same people often cannot express positive feelings at all. Passive people think that what they feel is unimportant so they, too, keep in their positive feelings.

Positive feelings range from saying "Thank you" to saying "I love you." There is a broad area that can be called positive regard: all those things that could begin "I like..." or "I appreciate...." Alice felt a positive regard toward Harold that he would have appreciated knowing about. She could have said, "Thank you, Harold, I appreciated your help all year," or "Your support has been real important to me. I'll miss you next year."

It is usually easier for girls to express positive feelings than it is for boys. Girls have been taught that it is all right for them to say nice things to people. It is okay for them to be "mushy." Boys find it more difficult to give compliments or say positive things, especially to each other, because of their ideas of what *real* men do. Besides, the other boy might think they were dumb for saying, "I really enjoy spending time with you." Yet, think of the times you received positive messages like that, and remember how you felt. It feels good to be on the receiving end. It is important to be on the sending end, too!

Alice had a feeling of dissatisfaction when she did not tell Harold how she felt. Not asserting positive feelings can be as frustrating as holding in negative feelings. Sharon Shy thinks Sam Server, who works in the cafeteria, is nice. He says hi to her and smiles and has her nachos all ready for her without her having to give him her order. He is in her English class, too, but Sharon just rushes by him with a shy smile and a whispered hi. She would like to tell him that it is really nice to have special service in the cafeteria, but she cannot. Sam is just waiting for a little encouragement from Sharon; he thinks she is cute and would like to take her out. Poor Sharon and Sam may never get together because neither one can express their positive feelings toward the other.

Vernon Vexing has had some hard times at school and at home. He has been seeing Mr. Mentor, his school counselor, for several months now and has made some major changes in his behavior. Things at home look a little different now, and Vernon sees that his parents were not always as wrong as he thought they were. Letting his parents know the change in his feelings and how he views them would help the relationship a lot. Vernon has practiced what he wants to say with Mr. Mentor, and he promises at every session that he is going to tell his parents, but he just cannot seem to do it.

If Vernon's parents do not express their positive feelings, Vernon's difficulty is understandable. He has not been taught how to communicate positive feelings. Vernon is not sure how his feelings will be received by his parents, and he cannot risk ridicule or rejection. Sharon and Sam share his feeling of rejection, and Alice does not want to take a chance on sounding foolish.

Expressing positive feelings begins with simple assertions like these: "I like your blouse." "Your hair looks good that way." "I like your sense of humor." "I enjoy your company." "That color looks great on you." "Your friendship is important to me." "Thanks for helping." "I'm glad you got the award, you deserved it." "You play the piano very well." "Thank you for spending the day with me." "Your speech was the best of all." "I like you."

Practice saying positive things to people who are not close to you. Tell a stranger in a store that you like her blouse (his shirt). Tell a boy in the hall that you like his sweater. Tell a teacher that she looks especially attractive today. Tell a teacher that his lecture was interesting (but only if it was). Thank the school secretary when she gives you an admit slip. You will soon find that saying positive things comes easier. Then it is time to move to the more personal things with people you care about. Tell your mom that you love her. Tell your dad that you appreciate the time he spends with you. Tell your best friend that he is important to you. Begin to free yourself by expressing your positive feelings.

When You Want to Let People Know What You Want Or Need

The fourth area of assertion that gives trouble is that of communicating your own wants and needs. It would be so nice if everyone could guess what you want, and you would not have to tell them. Kevin Kombat's dad thought Kevin needed some cheering up, but he guessed wrong. Kevin was really suffering, but he could not say, "Dad, I really need to be alone for a while." His dad would have understood, but Kevin thought (and *he* guessed wrong) that he might hurt his dad's feelings if he said that. Playing "Guess what I'm feeling" never pays off, but Kevin has not seen or heard many people express their wants or needs directly.

As Suzie Scholar was working on her English term paper, she realized that Phyllis Friendly had borrowed her booklet that showed the form for footnotes. Suzie needed the booklet in order to finish. It was only six o'clock, so she decided to call Phyllis. When she called, Phyllis had not finished her paper but was planning to work on it later in the evening. Suzie had been working on being more assertive, so she said, "Phyllis, I understand that you want to keep the booklet until later, but I need it right now. I'll be over to get it in a few minutes." Suzie did not get into a discussion with Phyllis over whose needs were greater or more important. She expressed understanding for Phyllis, stated her own needs, and made arrangements to take care of the matter. It saved hoping that Phyllis would offer to return the booklet or arguing over who should have it.

Sometimes you have a need for special understanding from a friend. Instead of waiting for the friend to ask what is wrong and going through the whole routine of "Nothing. I'm sure there is; please tell me," express your needs. "I feel really bad and I need a friend to listen to me," or "I feel so bad I just need somebody to be with me."

Some people have difficulty expressing very simple wants or needs. "I want to go home now," may come out as, "Don't you think it's time we left?" A call home that starts out, "You gotta come and get me," may make a parent say, "I don't have to do anything of the kind." When the same parent hears, "I need a ride home," the reaction is very different. Decide what your need is and state it:

"I need more quiet to get my work done."
"I need time to get to know you before I go out with you."
"I want to stop for lunch now."
"I want to ride in the front seat tonight."
"I would like to invite a friend to dinner Saturday."
"I need to know how much the tickets will be."
"I have a problem and need some help with it."

Stating wants and needs up front saves wear and tear on everyone. You do not have to hint around, hoping people will guess what you need. You need not be disappointed because they guessed wrong, and they need not be confused because you are acting strangely.

People Who Cause You to Feel Nonassertive

Not only situations may cause you to feel nonassertive, but also people. Perhaps you deal with strangers well but allow close friends to take advantage of you. How do you deal with authority figures such as parents, teachers, school administrators, or police? How do you handle peers, members of the opposite sex, people you want to like you? All of the people in your life have influence

over you. You react to them according to how significant they are
to you. How you react to them is important. When you cope with
your little brother, are you aggressive? When Mr. Neighbor tells
you to stay off his lawn, do you react aggressively and tell him you
will walk wherever you please? Look at the list of people in Table
1 and check the ones who are a part of your life. Think of how you
usually react to them—passively, aggressively, or assertively—and
do not confuse aggressive and assertive; you know the difference.

TABLE 1

	Passive	Aggressive	Assertive
Mother			
Father			
Grandparents			
Other adult relatives			
Brother/sister			
Cousins			
Teachers			
Administrators			
School staff			
Neighbors			
Boss			
Other adults			
Police			
Other authorities			
Friends			
Other peers			
Aggressive peers			
Opposite sex			
People you want to please			
Strangers			
Younger children			

To make your survey complete, you need to decide in which
areas of assertion you have difficulty with these people. Perhaps
you cannot express negative feelings to friends, but you can to
family members. In the area of wants and needs, you may not do
well with anyone on the list. Maybe you can express positive

feelings to your grandparents and your mother, but not to your father and sister. Using Table 2, check the areas of assertion in which you have difficulty.

TABLE 2

	Saying No	Expressing Negative Feelings	Expressing Positive Feelings	Expressing Wants and Needs
Mother				
Father				
Grandparents				
Other adult relatives				
Brother/sister				
Cousins				
Teachers				
Administrators				
School staff				
Neighbors				
Boss				
Other adults				
Police				
Other authorities				
Friends				
Other peers				
Aggressive peers				
Opposite sex				
People you want to please				
Strangers				
Younger children				

When you have completed your survey, you will know in which area and with which people you need work on coping more assertively. If you are aggressive with your sister and have difficulty expressing positive feelings toward her, you could begin by being less aggressive (perhaps stop calling her names) and by saying something positive to her. Keep your survey for future reference so you can use it to help you set goals for progress in coping more assertively.

CHAPTER IV

Coping with Yourself

Terry Timorous is reading a notice for a school ski trip. She has always wanted to learn to ski but has never had the opportunity. She knows that Alice and Fred and Melody ski and are planning to go on the trip. Terry cannot decide if she should go, and she is not sure if she should ask the others about it. She stands by the door of the activities office debating in her mind. "Everyone says skiing is a lot of fun. Yeah, but they all started years ago. They're all good skiers. They wouldn't want to bother with me. Besides, I'm so uncoordinated I'd probably fall down a lot and everyone would laugh at me and that would be awful. If I knew I wouldn't look stupid, I'd go. Oh! I don't have any ski clothes. Maybe I could borrow some from Melody or Alice. If they mention the trip, I'll tell them I'm thinking about going, and maybe they'll offer to lend me something. If they offer and the clothes fit, then maybe I'll sign up."

Terry is doing a great job of talking herself out of something she would really like to do. The Voice in her head is making it almost impossible for her to go on the trip. You have a Voice like Terry's talking to you all the time. There is a constant dialogue between you and the Voice. Most of the time you do not notice it because it is underground and automatic; but it determines your behavior, feelings, and self-esteem. The Voice is your judgmental self. It keeps the Real You blocked and forced out. The Real You is deep inside where your feelings are, and it is your best friend. The Voice works against the Real You.

The Voice comes from all the people who influenced you as you grew; the ones who taught you to play the Great American Games. The Voice takes over where the real people leave off and becomes your mother, father, grandfather, teacher, friend, neighbor, enemy, or whoever it decides can keep you from listening to the Real You. The Voice tells you who and what you are. It gives you your self-image.

Your self-image is based on the picture of yourself you have received from others. If significant people in your life called you a klutz and told you that you were stupid, you believed them.

35

Whenever you carry something and it spills, the Voice reminds you that you are clumsy and that is what is to be expected from a klutz like you. If your grade is lower than your parents expect, the Voice tells you it is because you are stupid. If significant people in your life were supportive, the Voice will be more supportive. However, the Voice prefers to let in negative things rather than positive things. It will remember that your uncle told you that you talk too loud, that your neighbor said you were irresponsible, that your cousin said your ears were too big, and that your dad said you were too small to play sports. Your grandmother may tell you that she appreciates how dependable you are about mowing her lawn, but the Voice tells you that you are irresponsible. Friends may tell you that your eyes are beautiful, but the Voice tells you that your ears are too big.

The Voice will ignore the positive and go right for the negative. The one wrong note you played in the concert is the one the Voice tells you about. Nothing less than perfection is acceptable to the Voice. When you have been in a discussion with someone you respect, the Voice will tell you all the stupid things it thinks you said but not the good points you made and the knowledge you shared.

The "shoulds" in your life come from the Voice and make you go against the feelings of the Real You. It tells you not to trust the Real You because you "shouldn't" feel that way. Whenever you want to be assertive, the Voice will say things to stop you.

Terry's Voice really did a number on her. It called her names, told her that terrible things would happen, and made demands that were almost impossible to meet. No wonder she could not decide what to do. Inside your head your Voice uses what Pamela Butler in *Talking to yourself* calls "stoppers" that confuse you and keep you from your natural, healthy assertiveness.

Negative Labels

The labels you put on yourself tell you what you think of yourself. That Terry thought the others would not want to bother with her indicates that she considers herself unimportant and a nuisance. Even though she is a good dancer and plays the piano well, she calls herself uncoordinated because she cannot catch or throw a ball very well. Terry's own view of herself appears to be somewhat unrealistic, but Terry believes what the Voice tells her.

Your Voice has labels for you that will stop you in all four areas of self-assertion: expressing positive feelings, expressing negative feelings, saying no, and telling other people your wants and needs.

Oscar wanted to tell Billy that his comments were unnecessary, and the Voice said, "Don't be a troublemaker." Suzie wanted to tell Tracy Carbon that his request made her feel uncomfortable, and the Voice said, "Don't be so touchy." Phyllis Friendly wanted to tell Ruby Roarer that it had been rude to accuse her of having cooties, and the Voice said, "Don't be bitchy." Fred wanted to tell the girls that he did not want to go to the dances, and the Voice said, "Don't be mean." Patsy wanted to tell Vicky Victim that she could not have a ride, and the Voice said, "Don't be unkind."

When Terry wanted to answer the request in the bulletin for someone who played the piano well, the Voice said, "I'll sound conceited." When Kevin Kombat wanted to tell his dad that he needed to be alone, the Voice said, "Don't be selfish." Everyone was stopped from doing what each had every right to do. They all judged themselves negatively for their natural human impulses, and once judged, they felt they would be doing wrong by asserting themselves.

Negative labels not only keep you from asserting yourself, but also squelch your creativity. Whenever you want to get involved in a new activity, the Voice begins. Terry could not learn to ski because she was uncoordinated. Oscar almost did not accept the job at Big Sky because he was too green. When Suzie was asked to write a column for the local paper, the Voice told her she was too inexperienced. Any new experience brings out the Voice, and it says "I can't because I'm ..." and lays on a label that can stop you before you even start.

When you are enjoying yourself the Voice can start up and ruin your day. Alice was on the ski trip and having a great time until she rode the lift with a guy about twenty-five. He was making comments that Alice thought were offensive. She wanted to tell him that she did not like his raunchy remarks, and the Voice said, "Don't be so thin-skinned; it isn't important." Alice did not say anything to the guy, but all day she argued with the Voice. She kept thinking of what she should have said or could have said or would have said. "If it hadn't sounded bitchy, I woulda said ... If it wasn't mean, I coulda said ... I shoulda said ... but it woulda been rude." Alice got caught up in shoulda, woulda, and coulda, and it put a shadow on her day.

Some positive-sounding labels can get you into uncomfortable spots, too. Sometimes trying to live up to being a nice guy, a good student, a good person, a sweet kid, a good friend, can make it impossible to say no or to let other people know that you have negative feelings. Nice guys do not tell friends that they cannot borrow their tapes. A good friend always listens on the phone even if it means being late for a dance committee meeting. A sweet kid never gets upset when someone borrows her notes and then lends them to five other people. A good daughter baby-sits her little brother and sister and does not tell her mother that there are play try-outs, and she loses her chance to be in the play. "Good" labels can rob you of your assertiveness and allow others to infringe on your rights.

The labels you put on yourself are usually not based on truth, honesty, or reality. Good friends do not expect their good friends to listen and be late for committee meetings. It is not conceited to tell yourself and others that you play the piano well if you do. It is not selfish to want to be alone. It is not bad to be inexperienced. You are not too thin-skinned when people have intruded on your rights.

Something Awful Will Happen

Another way the Voice stops you is by telling you all of the awful things that might happen. "If I fall down, I'll look stupid," was a big concern for Terry. Alice was afraid that Harold would think she was stupid if she told him how much she appreciated his help. Fred wanted to say no to the girls but, "What if their feelings are hurt?" The ending for a "What if" is "That would be awful." What if I look stupid? That would be awful. What if their feelings are hurt? That would be awful.

The Voice will tell you all the awful things that will happen if you assert yourself. Psychologist Albert Ellis calls this catastrophizing—imagining all the terrible catastrophes that might occur. You exaggerate the consequences until you cannot take the risk.

Randy Roarer has worked at a print shop for two years. He sweeps, loads boxes on the truck, and does whatever odd jobs need to be done. He has been paid the same wage since he started working there, when his only job was to sweep. Randy would like a raise, but whenever he thinks about talking to Mr. Litho, his Voice goes to work. "If I ask for a raise, Mr. Litho may think I don't appreciate having this job. He may think I don't like him because he isn't paying me enough. He may decide that since I don't appreciate the job and don't like him, he'd just as well fire me. Then I'll be out of a job, and I won't be able to use Mr. Litho for a reference, and nobody will hire me. I really need a job, so maybe I'd better not ask for a raise and just hope he decides to give me one."

Randy may not catastrophize to that extent, but he still could do a number on himself with one sentence. "What if I asked for a raise, and he turned me down?" Of course, the answer is, "That would be awful." Why would it be so awful for you to be turned down? You would feel embarrassed. Why would it be so awful if you looked stupid? You would feel embarrassed. Most of your "awfuls" are that you would feel embarrassed or your pride would be hurt. So what? It is worth the risk, because you might get that raise if you asked. It is worth the risk because you can have so much fun skiing that falling down would not matter. Most of the fears of embarrassment never happen, and if they do, so what? It is no big deal. You will stop yourself from living if you listen to your Voice and its catastrophes.

Unreasonable Demands

Terry will go skiing *if* she is sure she will not look stupid and *if* one of the girls will read her mind and offer to lend her some clothes and *if* the clothes fit. Those are heavy requirements to meet. If Terry makes the demands unreasonable enough, she will not go on the trip. Vernon Vexing will talk to his parents if the time is right, and you can be sure that the Voice will tell Vernon that there is never a right time. Sam Server's Voice says to ask Sharon Shy to go out if she talks to him after class. Sharon can hardly whisper hi on the way to her seat. It looks as if Sam is going to have a long wait until that demand of the Voice is met.

By setting up such unreasonable demands, your self-assertion is stopped. No matter what you might want to do or say, the Voice will set the requirements in such a way that you will not do or say what you need to. Fred would say no if it would not hurt the girls' feelings. Oscar would say something to Billy if it were absolutely necessary. Randy will ask for a raise if he knows Mr. Litho will say yes. Suzie will tell Tracy he cannot copy her homework if he will not be angry. All of the if's are unreasonable and are sure stoppers to any assertive expression.

Changing What the Voice Says

Becoming more supportive of yourself is no easy task, but a positive, supportive inner environment will make your world a much happier place. To accomplish that you need to ask yourself, "What am I telling myself?" Awareness that the Voice is talking to you is your first step to changing what it says. Conversations with the Voice are so much a part of you that you do not realize they are going on. You need to become aware of *when* you are saying negative things to yourself as well as what you are saying.

Become aware of your negative labels and get rid of them. You do not deserve to be called stupid, unimportant, uncoordinated, or any of the other labels. You may be uninformed but not stupid, a beginner but not a klutz, sensitive but not thin-skinned. Change those labels so that you are more supportive. Terry plays the piano well, and when the Voice wants to label her conceited, Terry needs to tell herself, "I am not conceited. I do play well." Fred needs to tell the Voice, "I am not being mean. I am honest." Terry needs to say, "I'm not uncoordinated; I'm a beginner."

Negative labels are not true or honest, and you do not have to accept them or believe them. You certainly do not have to keep repeating them. Change the negative labels to more supportive, positive labels.

Overcoming your Voice's catastrophes can be simple—not easy, but simple. You give yourself permission to be assertive "even if" the disaster happens. It is okay to go skiing even if I look stupid. It is okay to ask for a raise even if I get turned down. It is okay to tell someone "I do not like raunchy talk" even if they think I am thin-skinned. Tell yourself, "I am okay even if I'm not perfect; even if my friend gets angry; even if I feel embarrassed." Whatever your imagined catastrophe, you are okay even if it happens.

The unreasonable demands made by your Voice can be defused the same way. Sam can ask Sharon for a date even if she does not talk to him after class. Suzie can tell Tracy he cannot copy her homework even if he gets angry.

If you allow yourself to be stopped from expressing your true feelings, they will come out in some other way. Fred did not want to hurt the girls' feelings by saying no to them, but *his* feelings came out in his attitude during the evening. They were much more hurt by Fred's rejection during the evening than they would have been by a clean no in the beginning.

Stuffing your feelings cannot go on indefinitely without showing up. Besides blowing up when your gunnysack cannot hold any more, your resentment may come out in stomachaches, headaches, or other physical ailments. Rather than taking things out on other people by exploding, you take it out on yourself. You punish yourself for not being assertive. Also, the shyness you feel, the fear of exposure, can cause you to isolate yourself. You become so afraid to speak up that you find yourself all alone.

You may find yourself thinking and doing things to avoid situations and people. Some thoughts might be: "I wish I didn't have to go to school today." "I wish I had a million dollars, and I'd never have to work again." You may wash the car for your dad, clean the garage for your mom, take your dog for a walk, do all sorts of little jobs and find there is no time to talk to your dad about how embarrassed you feel having to take your younger sister and her date to the dance with you and your girlfriend. Your Voice is working overtime keeping you busy so that you will not have to confront the issue. Thoughts and behaviors that help you avoid asserting yourself are signs that you need to pay attention to.

Evaluate the Voice

When you become aware that the Voice is talking, ask yourself, "Is this helpful?" Do not ask if it is true or right or realistic. Just ask if it is helpful. Pay special attention to how it affects your feelings. Does it make you feel good? Does it make you feel free to assert yourself? Does it encourage you to take risks and grow and learn, or does it hold you back? Does it raise your self-esteem? If the Voice is not saying things that support you, that are helpful, that make you feel good about yourself and feel free to follow your feelings, you need to put a stop to the Voice.

After becoming aware of the Voice and what it is saying, you need to identify which stopper you are putting on yourself. Is it a negative label that is making you feel so bad? What imagined disaster have you come up with this time? Is it an unreasonable demand that you cannot possibly meet that is holding you back? Once you know how you are stopping yourself, the Voice loses a good deal of its power over you. You are able to change the label to a positive one or to tell yourself to go ahead even if the catastrophe happens or the demand is not met. You can create your own inner environment of support that is so vital to your positive regard for yourself.

As long as the Voice is running your life, you will not be able to accept positive regard from outside. You will not believe the good things other people tell you because the Voice will tell you that they are wrong. The Real You must take over management of your inner environment so that the positive support will keep the Voice quiet.

A Word About Aggressive Voices

It is not what happens; it is what you tell yourself about it that determines the significance. Three people can have three very different views of the same event. Rita Booker was skiing down the hill and passed under the ski lift. A skier on the lift shouted and waved to her. Rita just skied on without responding. The following three reactions could come from the lift rider, depending on the Voice of the individual.

> MELODY MODERATE: I guess Rita didn't hear me. I'll catch up with her later.
> PENNY PASSIVE: I wonder why Rita didn't wave. Maybe I did something to make her mad, and she doesn't want to talk to me.
> RUBY ROARER: Rita is sure getting stuck up. Well, see if I care whether she talks to me. I don't need to be friends with her.

Ruby's Voice has chosen to be angry because Rita "should" have waved. The conversation of the Voice was: "There's Rita. I'll wave and tell her I'll wait for her at the top. Well! She just skied right by and didn't pay any attention to me. After all the help I gave her when she was learning to ski last year, she should appreciate me more. Now that she has taken private lessons and skis the steeper slopes, she thinks she's big time. She can't snub me like that and get away with it. Whenever *she* feels like being friends, she comes around; but she doesn't really care about me, or she wouldn't be so stuck up. I don't know why I ever thought she'd be my friend. She always was a snob—lives in a big house, has her own car. Her folks hand her everything, and I have to work for every cent I have. She's totally selfish and thinks of no one but herself. Miss High and Mighty Rich Pitch is who she thinks she is. She looks down on poor trash like me. Well, who cares. I don't want to be friends with somebody like that anyway!"

Ruby has created her own monster. She decided what Rita was

thinking and got angry without even checking whether Rita had seen her. Since Ruby will avoid Rita in the future, Rita may never know why Ruby will not talk to her. Rita is completely innocent. She did not snub Ruby. She had her Walkman on, listening to music, and did not hear Ruby's yell. She would have been delighted to meet Ruby up top because she was tired of skiing alone and would have loved the company of someone who skied a little better than she.

Because of the Voice of anger and aggression in Ruby's head, the friendship may be lost. The negative labels Ruby put on Rita were not true and were unjust put-downs. Stuck-up, snob, unappreciative, big-time, rich pitch, are all labels that discredit Rita and anger Ruby. By her own labeling and with no action whatever from Rita, Ruby has ended up feeling humiliated and looked down on. That kind of Voice destroys relationships with others. Using the process for changing what the Voice says will work on aggressive Voices that make you angry as well as on Voices that stop you from following your natural inclinations. When you ask, "Is this helping?" your answer will be a resounding *no*.

You need to take a look at the things that anger you and see if you are the main cause of your anger. If you are angry because the traffic is moving slowly, where is that anger coming from? The Voice says: "This is stupid. I should have known better than to go down this street. Besides that, here I am stuck behind this turkey in the camper. He'll probably creep along at twenty miles an hour for miles. What are you honking at, Dummy? I can't move until this jerk goes!" In a minute the Voice will have you screaming obscenities and making rude gestures at people. When traffic is stalled, no matter what you do you cannot move it. Why get yourself into a rage? Does it help? No! Then tell your Voice to be quiet and say more supportive things to yourself rather than anger yourself while labeling other people.

If people are constantly angering you, check your own inner Voice and see if that may not be where the anger is coming from. Randy Roarer stood in line from ten in the morning until the gates opened at six to get a good seat at a concert. As he was going in the crowded gate, a guy pushed him pretty hard. "Hey, watch who you're pushin'," Randy said, and the Voice told him to push the guy back. "I can't let him get away with that!" Since the guy had not pushed Randy intentionally, he was angry; his Voice was just as aggressive as Randy's and told him that this dude had no business treating him that way and deserved to be taught a lesson in manners. Five minutes later they were sitting in the security office and were lucky to get off with a reprimand. Neither boy went to the concert that night.

Sometimes the Voice can hold a two-sided conversation, and you end up in a rage over what you have imagined the other person will say. "If I ask my dad if I can use the car on Friday, he'll say I haven't done all my chores around the house. I'll tell him I've done everything I'm supposed to do, and he'll remind me of some dumb, nit-picking thing that doesn't matter anyway. Then I'll tell him it's not fair for him not to let me use the car over something as stupid as that. Then he'll tell me not to talk to him in that tone of voice, and I'll tell him that he's yelling at me. Then he'll tell me not to say another word and to go to my room before I really get in trouble. He never listens to me, and he's always unfair. He always gets his way, and won't let me do anything. He makes me so mad!"

This whole episode did not even happen and you are furious with your father. You feel resentful and will carry that over with you when you actually do ask to use the car. Dad did not do a thing, yet he's the bad guy. This kind of talk from the Voice will distance you from people and keep you unnecessarily angry. Listen to your Voice to see if you are generating your own anger. Much of your aggressive behavior may be the result of what you have done to yourself by listening to an aggressive Voice.

CHAPTER V

Talking Assertively

Ben Evallent is the only one in his crowd who has a car to drive to school, so he gives rides to four other people. The agreement is that each give him $2.50 every Monday for gas. The last two Mondays Sharla Tun has not paid. The first time Ben figured that anyone could forget, but the second time that excuse was a little old. This morning when she got into the car for the third Monday in a row without paying, Sharla did not even offer Ben an excuse, let alone the $7.50 she now owed him. He was really mad. This was enough. He would not drive her to school if she was not going to keep her agreement to pay him. He had overlooked it long enough. Tomorrow he would just drive by her house and leave her standing there.

For two weeks Ben had been angry with Sharla. Every day he had expected her to pay him the money she owed, and every day when she did not, he had grown more angry. He did not ask her for the money, nor did he ask when she intended to pay him. He expected Sharla to say something when she saw the others pay him. He had barely spoken to her for the last week, and she should have gotten the hint. Ben did not say anything to the other riders, but they could tell he was angry with Sharla. They were not surprised when they asked where she was and Ben said she was not riding with them anymore. They did not want to seem nosy about what had been a personal thing between Ben and Sharla, so they did not ask either one what had happened.

Ben's nonassertiveness in coping with the situation with Sharla has led to very aggressive behavior on his part. He has ended up feeling angry and resentful toward Sharla, and unless he deals with her assertively, he is going to carry that resentment in his gunnysack for a long time. By communicating assertively, which has been defined as honestly, directly, and appropriately, Ben could have freed himself from the restrictions of his angry feelings.

Stating Feelings Directly

Stating feelings directly is just that; saying what you mean clearly to the person involved. Giving hints, hoping that they will guess, trying to manipulate things so they will get the idea, or any other indirect thing that you might do is not satisfactory. Remember, people usually guess wrong. You must say straight out what you feel, want, or need. Until you have said, "I need a ride home today," you cannot be sure the other person knows your need. If you are hurt by the way a friend has treated you and she seems uncaring, you cannot be sure you know how she feels until you say, "It hurt my feelings when you called me silly yesterday." You may be thinking, "I can't say that." If that is your reaction, listen to what the Voice is saying to you, because that is what is stopping you from being direct.

Asking Sharla to pay him was impossible for Ben. It was humiliating to ask for money, and Ben was angry that he was put in such a position. He had showed Sharla that he was angry, too. He had not talked to her, and he had not eaten lunch with her as he usually did. He did not, however, say, "I am angry because you haven't paid me." His Voice said that she should pay without being asked because asking for money is a humiliating, unmanly thing to do and he should not have to do it. Besides, if he went to Sharla and said, "When are you going to pay me for driving you to school?" she would think that he was greedy and grasping, and that would be awful. Even though Sharla was the one who violated Ben's rights by breaking their agreement, the Voice makes Ben feel he would be wrong to ask! Ben has every right to ask for his money.

It may be that Sharla would like to tell Ben why she has not paid him but is embarrassed because she owes him for three weeks. On the other hand, Sharla may have been taking advantage of Ben, figuring that he was such a nice guy that he would not ask her for the money. If he did ask she could just tell him she did not have the money and did not know when she would. He could only tell her that she could not ride with him any longer. It saved her $1.25 a day Municipal Transit fare she would have to pay otherwise.

By this time, getting paid is not the most important thing for Ben. Taking care of his feelings *is*. If Ben gunnysacks the issue, carrying a long-term resentment against Sharla is only part of what he will pay. He will feel victimized and used, and that is always paid for with loss of self-esteem. Ben cannot feel good about the way he handled the issue. The Voice might say, "I showed her," but the Real Ben would know that it was not handled well, and he would not feel good about himself.

Ben can cope with his frustrations very directly and appropriately by saying, "I feel uncomfortable about having to remind you, but you haven't paid me for your ride to school in two weeks. I'd like to be paid." That is not aggressive; it does not infringe on Sharla's rights, and it is very direct so it cannot be misunderstood. Sharla can react any way she chooses, and no matter how she chooses to behave, Ben is okay. He has handled his feelings directly and appropriately.

Being direct also means stating your wants and needs and not asking questions. So often you need a translator to figure out what is actually being said. Below are some questions and their translations.

Question	*Translation*
Do you want to have lunch now?	I'm hungry.
Do you really want to do that?	I don't want you to do that.
Are you doing anything Friday?	Would you like to go out on Friday?
Can you handle all that work?	I don't think you can handle all that work.
Isn't Mr. Scientific nice?	I like Mr. Scientific.
Do you plan to eat all of that?	I want some of that.
Doesn't Sam look good in that hat?	I like Sam's hat.
Are you finished?	I want to leave.
Isn't this a cute dress?	I like this dress.
Is that the way the pieces fit?	It is put together wrong.

Asking questions leaves you open for disappointments and surprises. If you ask someone, "Do you really want to do that?" and the answer is, "Yes, I really enjoy it," you have a hard time following it with "I don't want you to do that." When you ask a question instead of directly stating what you want, you put yourself in a position for the Voice to do a number on you. "It really makes me mad that she's doing that. She knows I don't want her to do it, and she's doing it anyway." At that point, another resentment goes in the gunnysack, or an argument begins because you were not direct.

Answers to some questions may leave you with your mouth hanging open in surprise. When you like Rita's new haircut and you ask, "What do you think of Rita's hairdo?" you may get the answer, "Those haircuts are the most ridiculous things I have ever seen. I can't imagine why anyone would cut one side of their hair real short and leave the other side long and sticking out." Whoops! That was not what you expected. The discussion you wanted to have about whether to cut *your* hair that way can wait for a more objective friend.

When you ask a question instead of directly stating your feelings, wants, or needs, you give away your power in the situation. "Don't you think you're driving too fast?" gives the power to the other person. He can answer no and leave you feeling awkward and frustrated. "I feel uncomfortable going so fast," keeps the power of the statement with you. The driver can then decide if he wants to keep you feeling uncomfortable or if he will slow down to a more comfortable speed for you. He does not feel defensive or angry with you because you did not tell him what to do but simply made him aware of your feelings at a very low level of muscle.

Direct assertions are not easy if your way has always been to stuff things in your gunnysack or to give hints and hope people guess right. You will have to think about what you want to say, and you will need someone to help you practice saying your assertions out loud. Become aware of your indirect behavior and begin to work on becoming more direct.

When you are not direct with people, you are depriving them of their right to know what is wanted of them. It is extremely frustrating to try to figure out the hidden meaning, decide what the other person wants, and then discover that the guess was wrong. You can avoid all of the misunderstanding and frustration by providing others with clear, direct messages.

Stating Feelings Honestly

To state your feelings honestly, you must say what you are really feeling. It is likely that you are in the habit of deciding what you should feel in the situation. If you have been operating on "shoulds," not only will you have trouble identifying your real feelings, but also stating those feelings will be even more difficult. "Shoulds" keep you from being honest. While you are busy figuring out how you should feel, you lose the true feeling. Fear of what others will think if you state your true feelings holds you back. Your Voice will say, "I can't tell her how I *really* feel. She'll never speak to me again."

Ben's fear of what Sharla would think helped him avoid dealing with his feelings. The anger he felt was covering up other feelings that he had as well, for as soon as he began to feel taken advantage of, he would get angry at being used. He did not want to feel how disappointing it was to have been treated so shabbily. It hurt. Ben's Voice told him at first that he should wait for her to pay him. Then his Voice changed and said, "She really makes me mad. I'll tell her she'd better pay me or I won't give her a ride anymore. But if I said that, she might get mad. I'll give her another day or two. I shouldn't hassle over money." Ben talked himself out of his true feelings of being angry about being taken advantage of.

Rather than being honest about his feelings and saying, "I feel taken advantage of," Ben withdrew from Sharla. He pulled back and closed off physically and socially by not speaking to her and by not having lunch with her anymore. Ben would not talk about the situation with any of the other riders, who were just as dishonest about their feelings as Ben was about his. They were confused and curious, but they pretended nothing unusual was happening. They could feel the tension building between Ben and Sharla, but they were not about to mention how uncomfortable they felt. Their Voices were saying, "I should just keep out of this. It's none of my business. It'll all blow over soon. I shouldn't feel uncomfortable anyway, nobody's bothering me." Their Voices were telling them what they should do and feel. The Real You in everyone was ignored and discounted.

Randy Roarer was one of the riders. He did not want to state his true feelings because he thought he would be too vulnerable if he did. He could not put his true feelings out for everyone to see because they might think he was stupid. Their low opinion and lack of approval would be crushing.

If you do not tell how you truly feel, how can you expect others to respect your feelings? If your "shoulds" are keeping you from knowing your true feelings, it is time for you to get rid of the "shoulds" and ask yourself, "How do I *really* feel?" Become aware of your own feelings.

Trusting your feelings is the basis of assertiveness. If you are a "should" person, you will tell yourself that your own feelings are wrong and you should feel a different way. When you do that, it is your Voice speaking; so tell your Voice, "Maybe I shouldn't feel angry because she probably didn't mean it, but I *do* feel angry." Trust your feelings; you have a right to them just as others have a right to their feelings. Take responsibility for your feelings and express them honestly and appropriately. You deserve to have your feelings respected, and others deserve to know what your true feelings are.

"I" and "You" Messages

To be assertive you must state your feelings honestly and directly without infringing on the rights of others, without accusing or blaming, and without put-downs. The most effective way to do that is with "I" messages. An "I" message states your feelings directly and honestly. "I am angry." "I feel anxious." "I resent being called a jerk." "I like the way you treat people." It is very powerful because you take complete responsibility for your own feelings. The opposite of an "I" message is a "you" message. "You make me angry." "You shouldn't say things like that." A "you" message gives the other person power over you or tries to take his power away. "You make me angry" means "You have power over me to make me feel angry." "I am angry" means the feelings are mine. I am responsible for them, and I am willing to take care of them. "You shouldn't say things like that" means "You do not know how to talk, so it is my job to tell you how to behave." It takes away the other person's power. "I resent being called a jerk" keeps your power and lets the other person know that you do not like his behavior. He still has his power to do what he wishes about his behavior without a judgment from you.

"I" messages keep you from aggressive name-calling and put-downs. "I am really disgusted and disappointed that my confidence was broken and Terry was told what I said," is quite different from, "You jerk! How could you tell Terry what I said? You broke my confidence. You really make me mad when you do that!" The "you" statement calls the other person names, accuses her of breaking confidence, and gives her power over your feelings of anger. You will definitely get a defensive, aggressive response to it, or else you will have totally crushed a passive person. The "I" message gives the person a chance to think of her behavior, and if she was not the one who broke confidence, she can say, "I'm mad, too. That was a low thing for someone to do." You will not have unjustly accused and will not have to apologize later for inappropriate behavior. If the person did break the confidence, you have treated her with dignity and respect; she knows exactly where you stand and will have to look at her own behavior, not yours.

An "I" message keeps you focused on the problem. A "you" messsage takes you on a trip away from the problem.

BIG SISTER: You took my sweater and got it all dirty, you little creep. You make me so mad when you take my clothes without asking.
LITTLE SISTER: You weren't home so I couldn't ask you, and I needed it right then.
BIG SISTER: That's my favorite sweater and you probably ruined it. You make me sick!
LITTLE SISTER: I didn't ruin your stupid sweater. You're just a selfish pig.
BIG SISTER: Don't call me a pig, you little scum bag!
LITTLE SISTER: Mamma... She called me a scum bag!

Big Sister's rights were violated, but guess who is going to be in trouble? Little Sister is the injured party now, and big sisters shouldn't treat little sisters that way. The whole argument could have been avoided by using "I" messages.

BIG SISTER: I am really mad that my sweater was taken without my permission.
LITTLE SISTER: You weren't home and I needed it right then.
BIG SISTER: I feel furious that it is dirty when I want to wear it.
LITTLE SISTER: Well, I forgot to put it in the wash.
BIG SISTER: I don't want you ever to take my things without asking me first, is that clear?
LITTLE SISTER: Well, what if you're not home?
BIG SISTER: Then the answer is no. I don't want you to take anything of mine unless I say it is okay.

Big Sister has not called Little Sister names or put her down in any way, but Little Sister knows Big Sister means business. Little Sister cannot accuse Big Sister of hurting her or mistreating her in any way. The rule governing borrowing is very clear, and Big Sister has maintained her power and has treated herself and Little Sister with dignity and respect.

The "I" message kept the focus on Little Sister's behavior. The

entire conversation was about the fact that Little Sister had taken
the sweater without permission. The behavior that was dealt with
was Little Sister's. In the argument with the "you" messages, Big
Sister violated Little Sister's rights, and the focus wound up on Big
Sister's behavior. Little Sister got off because Big Sister treated
her badly. "You" messages take the focus off the problem and
place it on the personalities involved. "You" messages make the
receiver feel defensive. Feel the differences between these "I" and
"you" messages:

You're wrong.	I disagree with you.
You embarrassed me.	I feel embarrassed.
You shouldn't yell at me.	I don't like to be yelled at.
You're always late.	I feel annoyed when I'm kept waiting.
You are disgusting.	I'm disgusted.

"You" messages put people on the defensive and frequently
bring an aggressive response:

> I'm not wrong. You're the one who's wrong.
> You're too sensitive. You get embarrassed over nothing.

A "you" message often is turned back on the sender, the sender
becomes defensive and aggressive, and the battle rages. Many
arguments can be avoided if you change your communication from
"you" to "I."

However, "I feel that you are wrong" is still a "you" message,
even though you started with "I feel." Leave the "you" out. "I
feel angry about . . ." is a safe beginning; then you are talking
about what happened and not about the person.

"I" messages make it possible for you to express your feelings in
an appropriate way without intruding on the rights of others. Your
gunnysack can be kept empty by using "I" messages as situations
occur. You can express positive and negative feelings, say no, and
let people know your wants and needs with "I" messages.

Having some good-feeling words for your "I" messages is
important. "I'm mad" is okay, but "I'm annoyed," "I'm irritated," "I'm furious," "I'm exasperated," "I'm enraged" repre-
sent varying degrees of angry feelings. You will send a clearer
message if you use more explicit words for your feelings. The
following words may be useful for your "I" messages:

aggressive
anxious
arrogant
bashful
bored
cautious
confident
determined
disappointed
disgusted
ecstatic
enraged
exasperated
frightened
frustrated
threatened
embarrassed
grateful
helpful
impressed
insignificant

guilty
hurt
idiotic
indifferent
interested
jealous
lovestruck
miserable
negative
pained
perplexed
prudish
regretful
sad
satisfied
nervous
enthusiastic
resentful
skeptical
infatuated
tender

shocked
surly
suspicious
sympathetic
turned-on
undecided
amused
ashamed
boastful
conniving
contented
cranky
delighted
domineering
eager
overworked
pressured
greedy
homesick
talkative
inspired

The following are examples of assertive "I" messages:

"I" messages to express feelings:
I am annoyed that the book wasn't returned.
I feel furious when I see an animal mistreated.
I feel helpless when I'm shouted at.
I feel puzzled by that reaction.
I feel ecstatic about being invited to the prom.
I am delighted to be here.
I feel miserable about losing your key.
I feel pressured to do more than I'm able to.
I am tempted to walk out right now.

"I" messages in direct assertions:
I don't want to go.
I don't agree with you.
I don't use drugs.
I don't want you to use my hair dryer.
I don't lend my clothes.
I don't like to be yelled at.

I want to go home now.
I enjoy your company.
I like you.
I admire assertive people.
I need help with algebra.
I need to be alone for a while.
I need to be listened to right now.
I have a problem, and I think you can help me.

"I" messages keep the focus on you and your wants and needs. That keeps you in control of yourself. You do not put your feelings on others as is done with "you" messages; you keep your feelings and responsibility for them yourself. "I" messages are nonjudgmental and keep your feelings very personally yours. You let others know how you feel and what is going on with you, yet you keep your identity; you keep your You. Because you stay with your true feelings, you do not get lost in the hassle around you. You stay out of hassles and own your own feelings, and you do not have to take on anyone else's. Keeping to an "I" statement keeps you in control.

It is not easy to change from "you's" to "I's." It takes practice. Compose two "I" statements for each area of assertion:

Expressing positive feelings.
Expressing negative feelings.
Saying no.
Expressing wants and needs.

After you have written your assertions, read them aloud to yourself. Next, get a friend to listen to you say your assertions. Finally, choose at least one of your "I" messages and say it to someone "for real."

Listen to people talk and notice how often "you" messages are sent and how people react to them. Become aware of how you react to "you" messages. More important, become aware of how many "you" messages *you* send.

Why Be Honest and Direct?

Communicating your feelings honestly and directly saves you from misunderstandings. No one has to guess what you are thinking or feeling. There is no need to try to figure out what was meant by a remark. There is no underlying meaning; you mean what you say. What a relief, not having to think up hints and hope people know what you mean. What a relief for people around you to know exactly what you mean.

Poor Penny Passive got trapped in her own passive game. At midnight Penny began to worry because she had to be home at 12:30. She was with Frank Lee so she said, "Don't you think it's getting late?" Frank replied, "Oh, no, it's early." Penny did not know what to do, because she was going to be late and Frank did not take the hint. All Penny needed to do was to say directly, "I need to leave because I have to be home at 12:30." Because Penny was not direct, she got home an hour late, and her parents were furious with Frank. Frank resented being snarled at over something he had not known about. Being direct would have saved Penny, Frank, and Penny's parents the angry encounter that made Frank decide that he would not take Penny out again.

When feelings are expressed honestly and directly, there is no resentment from stored-up grievances. Annoyances are taken care of as they occur. Because resentment does not build, there is no aggressive explosion as a result of passively stuffing anger and irritation into your gunnysack. You express your feelings appropriately and feel good about yourself. Ben was so filled with resentment that he behaved aggressively toward Sharla, and it affected his self-esteem. He did not feel good about how he coped with the situation. Honest, direct, appropriate communication would have made him feel good about himself.

Often people are not honest and direct because they do not want to hurt other people's feelings, as in the case of Fred Friendly and the girls he took to the dances. Because of Fred's barely hidden resentment over getting "stuck" with the dates, the girls were hurt far worse than if he had said no in the beginning. They thought Fred liked them when he agreed to take them out. Imagine how they must have felt as the evening wore on and Fred got more and more distant. Too often, those you try to save from hurt feelings end up feeling crushed because they hoped for more from you than you could give. Being honest with them to begin with may hurt them a little, but it saves them from greater hurts later on.

Finally, honesty and directness give you credibility with yourself. It is easy to get focused outside of yourself and forget that you are responsible for your own feelings and needs. When you focus on others, you blame them for your feelings. You blame them when your needs are not met.

"Randy made me so mad yesterday. He found out that I have room in my car to take his girlfriend to the game, and now I'm stuck with no date because Randy's girl is taking the space I was saving for a date," said Victor Victim. From his point of view, Randy is to blame because Victor does not have a date; Victor would not be angry except that Randy *made* him angry. Victor has given Randy his right to his own feelings, his right to say no, and his right to associate with people of his choosing. Victor is not accepting responsibility for his own feelings and needs. His actions are saying, "I don't like my world the way it is, but I can't do anything about it." Victor would have you believe that he is powerless over the situation. That is not true for Victor, and it is not true for you. You make your world what it is. You either take responsibility for it, or you give that responsibility to others. You may think that others have taken your responsibility for yourself away from you, but no one can take it unless you let go of it. Coping assertively, honestly, and directly with others allows you to keep your responsibility for your feelings and needs and for protecting your rights without taking responsibility for others' feelings and needs while protecting their rights. You retain your power, believe in yourself, and feel good about the way you run your life. You are credible and creditable to yourself.

CHAPTER VI

Using Body Language Assertively

Torey Nato stamped into the room, slammed her books on the table, planted her feet firmly on the floor, jammed her hands on her hips with elbows defiantly out, narrowed her eyes, clenched her teeth, stuck out her chin, and glared at her brother. Without a word being spoken, Torey let her brother know exactly how she felt. She was ready to tear him apart! Every part of her body signaled fury.

Regardless of what is said verbally, your body sends a message of its own. Much of this nonverbal communication is automatic; you do not know you are doing it. You talk with your body as well as your voice, but your voice itself sends other messages besides the words you say. Your tone of voice, the volume of your voice, and how quickly or slowly you speak all add to the message you are sending.

Torey was very conscious of the message she was sending, and her behavior was deliberate. That is not always the case. Sometimes your body sends out a message you are totally unaware of. If you wonder why someone will not take no for an answer, you may be doing what is suggested in the old song, "Your Lips Tell Me No, No, But There's Yes, Yes in Your Eyes." In this case, the nonverbal message detracts from the verbal message. You can add power to your verbal message when your nonverbal message is consistent with it. Your whole body speaks, each part separately and the whole collectively.

How the Face Talks

Facial expressions can be clear indicators of your feelings. Reading faces is learned at an early age. Mom frowning at you meant something was not right. A smile meant things were going well. You learned to read more feelings from faces as you grew. Theoretically, you could know what people are feeling by looking at their faces. Unfortunately, it is not that easy. People in our society learn to cover up their feelings by making their faces as expressionless as possible. Randy Roarer started working on turning his face off when he was in fourth grade, so now he can sit through any kind of tongue-lashing that an adult gives out and never move a muscle in his face. He freezes, and there is no way to know how he feels.

Too often, people feel betrayed by what their faces say. If someone says, "You should see the look on your face," you feel defensive. You wish the look on your face could not be seen. When your feelings show in your face and others make fun of you, it causes you to become stone-faced. When you know your feelings and are comfortable sharing them with others, you will find that you feel okay about having your feelings show on your face. An answer to the put-down about the look on your face could be, "If I look shocked, it's because I am."

When making assertions, the expression on your face can make you believable or cause you to be disregarded. Patsy Pushover's mother decided that Patsy would have to tell the next-door neighbor that she could not baby-sit on school nights because Mrs. Neighbor came home too late. Patsy went next door and said, "Mrs. Neighbor, I really hate to tell you this, but I can't baby-sit for you anymore on school nights. My mom is really mad because I didn't get home until 12:30 the other night." The entire time Patsy was speaking, she had a smile on her face. She did not look at all as if she hated saying it. She looked quite pleasant.

Kay Kind was very hurt when Kevin Kombat said he would meet her in the library to work on algebra, and he did not show up. Kay was telling her good friend Melody Moderate about it. Kay said she was disappointed and felt embarrassed about seeing Kevin again because she would not know how to act. Although her words were serious and painful, she had a smile on her face that said, "Cancel out all that stuff about how down I feel. I didn't mind at all." Kay's facial expression and her words did not match. The smile lessened the power of the verbal message. Some people even add a giggle while they are telling some painful thing that has happened to them. It is a nervous habit that covers the pain and satisfies the Voice that says, "Nobody wants to listen to that from you. It's no big deal. Don't be so serious. You shouldn't feel that way." The smile makes it easier to dismiss the hurt if the listener is not sympathetic. If you are angry, a smile lessens the tension that is associated with anger. Unfortunately, it also minimizes the effect of the message.

A smile can be used to mask a very aggressive message. When Scott Scoffer smiled and said, "Oh, Tracy is a great passer. He can throw the ball anywhere on the field. There's just never anybody around to catch it where he throws it," he was not kidding. He meant to put Tracy down. Cruel, sarcastic remarks are often explained away as "just kidding" because the person delivering the message was smiling.

Your entire face works together to confirm or to cancel your verbal message. When Kay Kind said, "Oh, how nice," but looked as if she were smelling something bad, it was difficult to believe her words. A wrinkled brow tells you that some heavy concentration is going on unless the clenched jaw along with it says the person is angry. Arched eyebrows help you say you are surprised or excited. One eyebrow raised may very well signal trouble ahead. A smile that moves just the mouth and not the rest of the face is probably not sincere. Your face tells a story that can enhance your verbal story or cancel it out altogether.

Getting your face and mouth to work together is very important. If your assertive statement is, "I'm disappointed that we can't go to the movie," do not smile as you say it. If you are not sure that your face and words agree, ask a friend. Check to see if you laugh while making serious statements. Unless your facial expression and verbal message agree, you confuse people and they do not know which message to believe.

How Posture Talks

The *Random House Dictionary* defines posture as the position or carriage of the body as a whole. Torey Nato's entire body shouted anger to her brother. From head to foot she was furious. The way you use your body expresses what you are feeling. There are words to describe ways of walking that show how you feel. Randy Roarer often *swaggers* because he is showing that he is rough and tough. His shoulders are back, his head is up, and his arms are out from his sides. Patsy Pushover usually *trudges* along with her head down, shoulders drooped, and arms wrapped around her books. She looks weighed down. Even if Patsy says things are fine, you do not believe her. Rita Booker seems to *saunter* along, never in a hurry, with her head up, shoulders straight, arms relaxed, and she appears ready for whatever might happen.

Sitting down, you send a message. If you sit straight and lean forward a little, you say, "I'm listening. I'm interested." Leaning back, arms across the back of the sofa, you say, "I'm relaxed and paying attention." Slouched down, legs sprawled out in front of you, arms folded, head down, you say, "I'm not listening to you. I'm not interested. Go away." You may verbally say you are listening, but your body says you are not. Sitting up, feet on the floor, hands on the arms of the chair, you say, "I'm not staying here very long. I want out." Until you relax in the chair a little bit, the girl you are visiting is going to stay anxious about how you and her dad are getting along.

How you stand tells a story about you, too. Patrick Pushover always seems to stand near something, as though he wants to melt into the wall. His shoulders droop, he slumps in the middle, and his neck pushes his head forward just a little. He looks as if he will fold up and disappear into the floor. Fred Friendly stands in a loose, relaxed way. He has his left foot slightly in front of the right and sometimes rests a hand lightly on his hip when he is not using it to emphasize what he is saying. Kevin Kombat seems to be moving all the time. If he is just standing around, his arms are moving, and he shifts weight from foot to foot. He is always looking around and seems primed for action.

It is difficult for Patrick to be convincing even if he says the exact same thing as someone else. When Kevin dances up in front of the line and takes cuts on Patrick, even if Patrick says, "There are no cuts in line," Kevin will not believe him. One look at Patrick's sagging shoulders and Kevin knows Patrick will not put up any opposition that cannot be handled with a little bluster. An assertive statement is of little use without an assertive body stance.

How Hands and Arms Talk

Your hands and arms have messages of their own. Torey's hands jammed on her hips with her elbows defiantly out sent a very clear message. Clenched fists signal anger. Fidgety fingers say you are nervous. Drumming fingers say you are impatient or bored. You may say everything is fine, but if you put your hand up with your palm outward while you are talking, you are signaling "no" or everything is not all right. It is hard to convince someone you are interested in what he is saying if you are drumming your fingers on the table.

What you do with your hands while you talk can speak for you. If you do not think hands are important, get up to speak in front of a group and see how unimportant they are! If your hand keeps wandering up to cover your mouth, it lessens the impact of what you are saying. Finger-pointing and table-pounding add aggression to any statement. You may smile and say, "Your little brother is certainly active," but your clenched fist says you would like to smack the brat. You may think you are really cool and no one knows how you feel, but your white-knuckled hand on the arm of the dentist's chair gives you away. If you are at a movie with a girl who has both arms tightly wrapped around herself, you know she is not going to welcome your arm around her unless she is trying to keep warm; but be sure to ask if she is cold before you try to warm her up!

Your hands and arms are an important part of your communication process. It is not always what you say, but what you do while you say it, that gets the message across. To add power to your assertions, you must give the same message with your hands and arms as you do with your words.

How Your Feet Talk

How you walk and stand depend on your feet and legs, and your legs and feet can send messages of their own as well. Sally Simmer usually does not say much when she is irritated. However, Frank Lee has been a good friend of hers for a long time, and he knew she was really ticked off at Vernon. Sally was sitting across from Frank with her legs crossed, and as Vernon was talking, Sally began to kick her leg. Frank could tell how Vernon was affecting Sally because the angrier she got, the faster the leg went.

Kevin Kombat was usually moving. He hardly ever stood still, so when he stood in the middle of the hall, flat-footed with his legs slightly apart, everyone knew something was up.

Shifting weight from one foot to the other, Rita Booker stood waiting for the office door to open. Since she had heard about the job with this veterinarian, she had been excited, and now that the time for the interview was here, her nervous excitement was hard to control.

With one arm braced against a tree, Harold Helper stood there kicking at the dirt. With a final full, decisive kick, he walked off, determined to do something about this whole nothing with Alice.

Anger, excitement, and confusion are all shown through "footwork." Sally can say, "I'm not mad," but Frank knows better. Kevin is not trying to cover up what he is feeling; he is just waiting for that little twirp to say one more word. Rita will go in the door and be as calm as possible, but Dr. Woof will feel some of the excitement she has been showing in her feet. In the language of the body, feet have a story to tell.

What the Voice Says

Your tone of voice, more than any other factor, colors what you say. Young people tend to get into more difficulty as a result of the tone in which they say something than what they say. For example, you can say, "All right," and mean many different things. Ima was excited when Tracy asked her out and said, "All right," in a breathy tone. Fred skied down a run he had never conquered before and shouted, "All right!" in triumph. Ruby was tired of listening to her mother nag and snarled, "All right!" Ima's "All right" made Tracy feel excited; Fred's "All right!" made everyone else cheer; and Ruby's "All right!" made her mother snap, "Don't use that tone of voice with me, young lady!"

The voice tone of many young people is very aggressive. Much of the time you order each other around. You may start the sentence, "Why don't you ..." but the tone is the ordering tone you hate to hear from your parents and teachers. So often there is an edge in the voice that says, "I dare you to say something about it."

Many times young people run into trouble with older people because they use the same tone of voice as they do with their friends. The older people do not like the ordering, demanding tone of voice, and conflict occurs. A good way to discover your own tone of voice is to tape record some of your conversations with friends and also with older people, if possible.

The tone of voice may change when girls talk to boys on an individual basis. The girl's voice tends to be softer and more inviting. She wants to sound alluring and attractive. She may say things to flatter the boy and make him feel important. (She may even ignore her girlfriends while she makes a fuss over a boy she is interested in.)

Most girls do not realize that they use a different voice when they talk to boys. With the cover of the voice, a girl stops being honest and direct. It is as though the Voice inside says, "You'd better be careful and not do anything to make him mad, and you'd better not let him know how you really feel, or he may not like you anymore." She gives up her power and her responsibility for herself because she wants him to like her, and her true feelings are exchanged for what she "should" do to please him. When she talks to him, it is in that male-pleasing tone of voice that says, "You're so wonderful. I'll adore you if you stay near me."

Boys also have a different tone for talking to girls. The boy wants to show that he is the protector. He has to sound hip, slick, and cool as if he knows what's happening. It is equally hard for him to be honest and direct. How can he be hip, slick, and cool and let her know he is nervous or excited about going out on Saturday?

Shy people tend to change their voice tone when talking to the opposite sex. They lose any evidence of confidence in the voice. The tone has no authority whatsoever. It is very painful, and many such people, like Sharon Shy and Sam Server, avoid talking because it is so difficult.

The volume of your voice is very important in sending a message. Many of you tend to be loud when you get together. Girls tend to become quite shrill. Boys' heavier voices seem to rumble in a loud roar. That is fine when you are with a group of young people and everyone is talking loud. However, you need to consider the appropriateness of that volume in other places and with other people.

A loud voice sounds very aggressive. You can batter people with the loudness, and they will want to stay away from you to avoid being pounded by your voice. Other aggressive people will take the loud voice as an invitation to a fight, physical or verbal. If you use your loud voice to overpower people and get your way, do not be surprised that few people want to be near you.

On the other side are the people who speak so softly that you can hardly hear them. They are afraid to speak out. The Voice tells them, "Nobody wants to listen to me. Nobody is interested in my opinion. I'm usually wrong, so I won't say anything. If I have to speak I'll hope nobody hears me." It is very difficult for a genuinely shy person to speak assertively because the voice volume does not correspond to the assertion, and the power is lost.

Some people use a soft voice volume to control others. If you speak softly, others must listen carefully to hear you. You are in control and have others straining to catch what you are saying. Also, a soft voice volume can be very menacing. Dirty Harry did not shout. He very softly said, "Go ahead. Make my day."

A third quality of voice is the speed at which you speak. Patsy Pushover keeps getting stuck doing things she does not want to do because she does not talk fast enough. She hesitates with lots of uh's and ah's, and before she knows it the other person takes her hesitation for agreement. Part of what makes up your speech rate is the "filler" words you use. "Ya know," "man," "basically," "totally," "um," are all things you say to fill in pauses in your speaking. In fact, they may make pauses where none would naturally be. "I, ya know, uh, really think, ya know, uh, you were real good, uh, ya know, in the play," is a good try at a positive assertion, but it gets lost in the middle of the "ya know's." The power is lost. When someone cuts in front of you in the line at the bank, you can politely and assertively say, "The end of the line is back there." With the fillers, by the time you say, "Uh, excuse me, ah ... uh ... ya know ... the end of the line ... basically is back ... uh ... there," the person is already at the teller's window.

Effective use of your voice to give the message you want to communicate includes tone of voice, voice volume, and rate of speaking. All must say the same thing as the verbal message you are giving. Using a tape recorder to check your voice will help you become more consistent in your communication.

How Eyes Talk

Your eyes send out strong messages. They dance when you are happy and fill with sadness when you are not. They snap with anger and sparkle with enthusiasm. Eye talk is very important to your assertive communication. Where you look, how you look, and when you look will either help your message or destroy its effect.

Eye contact—looking directly at the other person and making contact with his eyes—is vital to assertive communication. Nonassertive people look down a great deal. They seldom really look at you. Whenever Penny Passive talks in the group at lunch, she looks at her hands or out of the window or at the ceiling or almost any place rather than at the faces of the people she is talking to. Sharon Shy does fine with her girlfriends; it's boys and teachers she cannot look at. Fred Friendly gives a lot of good eye contact to people his own age, teachers, his parents, his boss, almost everybody—but when his grandparents are around he has trouble. He wears his hair below his ears, and his grandparents say something about it every time he is around them. Fred finds it difficult to make eye contact with them.

When you look away from someone with whom you feel uncomfortable, it helps you feel less anxious. When Mr. Zero is unhappy with you for not doing your math homework, looking at the floor is much easier than making eye contact with him. When you want to tell Mr. Zero that you felt humiliated at being called dummy in front of the class, it is difficult to make eye contact.

In being assertive, it is important to look directly at the person to whom you are speaking and to maintain eye contact for a short time after you have finished. However, too much eye contact can be aggressive. People your own age may be intimidated by your steady stare. People older than you will be infuriated by the same stare. Maintaining eye contact beyond what is necessary says, "You're going to have to look down first; there is no way you are going to get the best of me and make me look down."

Lack of eye contact is usually nonassertive, but it, too, can be aggressive. Vernon Vexing used to infuriate his dad, and that is what Vernon wanted to do. He pretended that what he was doing was meant to keep his dad from getting to him and making him angry. He felt he was defending himself. When his dad would begin to get on his case, Vernon would put on a blank expression and look steadily over his dad's left shoulder. Mr. Vexing would get so angry that he would send Vernon out of the room to keep from hitting him. Vernon always felt that he had won, and he did it without saying a word.

Eye contact is a powerful part of your nonverbal communication system. Being aware of how you use eye contact or your lack of it is important for you. Become conscious of your need for eye contact and monitor yourself. Better yet, feedback from a friend or an adult you trust is a good way to find out the quality of your eye contact.

Using Body Language Assertively

Carrie Cadger was always borrowing things from people after P.E., including personal grooming items such as comb, lipstick, mascara, even deodorant. Patsy, Ruby, and Melody decided they had had enough. The three of them resolved to say, "I am not lending you anything more. Please don't ask again." The first person Carrie approached was Patsy, who was standing by the mirror combing her hair. Her purse was open, and the contents were clearly visible.

CARRIE: Hi, Patsy. Is that watermelon-flavored lip gloss?
PATSY: (With an unsure expression on her face.) Uh, yeah.

CARRIE: Oh, that's my favorite flavor. Can I use it? (Reaching for it.)
PATSY: (Shoulders drooped, looking down at the floor.) Well, uh ... I'm not ... uh ...
CARRIE: (Putting on the lip gloss.) Thanks, Patsy.

No matter what Patsy had said, Carrie would read the nonverbal "Do whatever you want, I don't count." Patsy's face showed her hesitance. She looked down as soon as she started talking, which told Carrie not to listen to her, and her voice was so low and halting that Carrie totally disregarded any verbal message. Patsy was treated disrespectfully by Carrie and by herself.

Later, in the cafeteria, Carrie sat down beside Ruby. Ruby had already eaten lunch and was looking through her biology notes.

CARRIE: Are those your biology notes?
RUBY: Sure are.
CARRIE: You always take good notes, Ruby.
RUBY: (In a loud voice, looking Carrie straight in the eye.) You bet I do, honey, and I am not lending my notes to you. I am not lending anything to you any more! (Slamming her hand on the table, gathering up her books, and stomping off.)
CARRIE: Wow! What brought that on?

It is likely that Carrie will steer clear of Ruby for a while. Ruby's aggressive nonverbal communication was overwhelming for the situation. The loud voice and aggressive eye contact were surprising enough to Carrie; but the pounding hand and huffy way Ruby stalked out were observed by almost everyone in the cafeteria. They all wondered what was going on. Ruby did not treat Carrie or herself with dignity and respect.

Right after school, Melody was standing by her locker, and Carrie walked up looking concerned.

CARRIE: Oh, hi, Melody. Boy, am I in for it if I don't find some white shorts by tomorrow. Everybody has to wear white shorts and a school T-shirt for cheerleading tryouts tomorrow. You're the same size I am. Do you have some white shorts you could lend me?
MELODY: (In a calm, firm voice, looking directly at Carrie.) I am not lending you anything anymore. Please don't ask again.

CARRIE: Well, uh, oh, all right. Are you mad or something, Melody?
MELODY: (In the same calm tone.) No, I just don't want to lend my things to you anymore.
CARRIE: Oh.

Melody was very direct. She stood firmly on both feet, looked at Carrie with a serious expression on her face, and made her assertion in a firm, calm voice. She did not put Carrie down. She did not try to blow Carrie away. Melody's message was clear and consistent because her verbal and nonverbal messages said the same thing. Carrie had no reason to be angry with Melody, but if she were angry, it would be okay. Melody handled herself well and treated Carrie with dignity and respect.

What could Patsy do to be more assertive with Carrie? She definitely wanted to do something, so she asked Melody to help her. Melody knew how difficult it was for Patsy because she could remember when she was having the same kinds of problems as Patsy. She had gone to see Mr. Mentor, and he had helped her with what she wanted to say and had practiced with her until she felt confident. Melody suggested to Patsy that they practice how Patsy would handle the situation.

The assertive statement was, "I don't want to lend my things to you." The first time Patsy said, "I uh . . . I don't want . . . uh . . ." Melody stopped her before she got any further. "You're speaking too softly. I can hardly hear you." After the second try, Melody told Patsy to say it without saying "uh". After the third try, Melody told Patsy to say it ten times louder. The fourth time, Patsy thought she was screaming, but Melody told her the volume was just right and to do it again.

All the time they were practicing voice volume, Patsy was looking at the floor. The next thing they worked on was eye contact. Patsy was so used to looking down that it was difficult for her to look at Melody. After working on the eye contact for a while, an interesting thing began to happen. Patsy began to stand straighter. Her shoulders lifted, and she looked as if she meant what she was saying. Melody encouraged Patsy to say her statement to Carrie the next time Carrie wanted to borrow something, and she promised to be standing by to lend moral support.

That night, Patsy practiced a few more times in front of the mirror. The next day she was scared, but ready.

CARRIE: I just ran out of deodorant. Can I borrow yours? (Reaching for the can.)
PATSY: (Picking up the can and looking at Carrie.) I don't want to lend you my things anymore.
CARRIE: (Puzzled.) Well, I'll give it right back.
PATSY: (Starting to look down but instead looking at Melody, who nods; looking back at Carrie.) I don't want to lend my things to you anymore.
CARRIE: Well, really! What's the big deal? (Turning and walking away.)

Patsy's heart was pounding, and the second time she made her assertion her voice had got softer, she had drooped just a bit, but the eye contact and the repetition of the same message got through to Carrie. Patsy knew that if she had to, she could do it again. She felt triumphant. She had not had to be mean; just to stand her ground. She stood taller the rest of the day. She gained dignity and respect for herself, and even though Carrie was miffed at Patsy, she was feeling respect for her, too.

It is a big jump from nonassertiveness to assertiveness. The Patsys cannot make that jump without bridging the gap, and a good bridge can be a school counselor or an adult or a friend who is assertive. If you are nonassertive, you need feedback from someone you trust, and you need practice.

Once you have your assertive statement, you need to consider how you sound and look when you deliver it. Practice making your assertion in a voice that matches the words. If you usually speak very softly, you may feel you are screaming when others think you are using a normal tone. That is why feedback from someone else is important. A tape recorder helps, but the Voice will begin judging if you are not careful. Another person to give feedback is best.

If you are alone, practice making your assertion in front of a mirror. Say it until you convince yourself that you mean what you say. How is your eye contact? Does your face agree with your words? What about the rest of your body? Does it say the same thing that your words do? Your body will speak for you even when you do not know it. Keep aware and use the nonverbal messages your body sends to strengthen your verbal message.

CHAPTER VII

Coping with Criticism

Tracy Carbon is usually pretty sure of himself, but when he is criticized for not catching a pass, he tries to find reasons for missing it. He will say Randy threw it short or the player on the other team was blocking his view of the ball. He will say that he slipped or that he had a sudden terrible pain in his side. Tracy always has reasons to justify the criticism.

When Frank Lee is told he never gets anything right just because he turned on the wrong burner of the new electric stove, he apologizes to his father and tells himself that he is dumb.

Patsy Pushover tries so hard to do well in Mr. Zero's class that she is completely crushed when he tells her that she got a D on the test because she did not put enough effort into her homework. She cannot say a word about the unjust criticism.

Randy Roarer practices football every day until 5:30 and works from 6 to 9 every night in the print shop, but he felt guilty when Mrs. Gibe said he was too lazy to get up early enough for the committee meeting to organize the can recycling drive that would pay for the Christmas food baskets for the needy. Randy told Mrs. Gibe that he gets more done in one day than her precious committee people do in a week, and Mrs. Gibe was so put off by his aggression that she did not care to find out that Randy is, indeed, a hard worker.

Kevin Kombat was getting a B in Spanish, and he knew that if he studied a little extra for his final, he could probably get an A. As he was leaving school the day before finals, Tracy Carbon asked him to go down and play video games at the arcade that night. Seeing the Spanish book in Kevin's hand, he said, "What's with the Spanish book, Kevin? You don't need to study. You'll be hanging around the Dexters before long if you're not careful." Kevin wanted to be "one of the guys," so he decided to go to the arcade instead of studying that night.

Reacting to Criticism

Those five reactions to criticism are typical of most people. Dealing with criticism is difficult because it is so personal. It attacks who you are inside. You may put up your defenses and try to act as if it does not really matter, but criticism—just or unjust, true or untrue—hits you where you live. You feel anxious and uncomfortable.

Having the approval of others is very important, and criticism says you are not perfect and are not approved of one hundred percent. If your happiness and well-being depend on approval from others, fear of criticism can keep you from being assertive. People can use your fear to manipulate you into doing what they want you to do. Criticism implies that you are wrong and the other person is right, or that what you are doing is wrong and there is a better way to do it. In either case, you feel a lack of approval from the other person. Even though you may know that what you have done is right for you, the criticism will cause you to question your judgment. If you are not assertive, it can cause you to change your behavior to please the other person and to go against your feelings.

Criticism from others can make you feel guilty because you think you must be wrong. You feel you are to blame; therefore, you must be guilty of something. Tracy felt guilty for missing the pass; Frank felt guilty for turning on the wrong burner; Patsy felt guilty for getting a D; Randy felt guilty for not being on the committee; and Kevin felt guilty for wanting to study. Nobody needed to feel guilty. Tracy and Frank were human and made errors; Patsy had done the best she could; Randy was already working hard; and Kevin had every right to get good grades if he wanted to. Other people used criticism to make them feel guilty. Much of the time the people doing that kind of manipulation do not realize they are doing it. It is another one of those things you learn early and do as an automatic response to situations.

In looking at the five responses to criticism, more is going on than you might notice on the surface. Tracy defended himself when the coach criticized him because he felt guilty and felt he had to have a reason for making a mistake. He felt that he had to be perfect, and when he was not, it was hard for him to admit it. He felt foolish and clumsy and could hardly listen to the coach telling him how to improve. The Voice in Tracy was already on his case, and criticism from the coach just made him feel more guilty. He wanted to cover up what he thought was a horrible defect, so he made excuses. The coach was not trying to make Tracy feel guilty, but when Tracy made excuses, the coach thought he was trying to avoid taking responsibility for his mistake. The misinterpretation of Tracy's behavior made the coach drive a little harder at him. It is important for Tracy to learn to cope with criticism from others and from himself so that he will not receive more criticism than is due him.

Frank Lee has a completely different problem dealing with the accusation that he never does anything right. Frank has been trying all week to stay on the good side of his father because the night he took Penny home late, the lecture from her parents made him late getting home, also. His dad was angry, and Frank was not sure when he would be allowed to use the car again. He wanted his dad's approval so that when he asked to use the car, there would be a better chance of getting permission. Frank's immediate apology for being so stupid was just the beginning of what his Voice told him about all the things he always does wrong. He thought of every dumb thing he had done lately, including not finding out what time Penny had to be home, which had put him in the fix he was in now. He was feeling very guilty about turning on the wrong burner and about making his father angry.

Frank's father had no idea how guilty Frank was feeling. Mr. Lee did not realize that he was heaping guilt on his son by saying, "Why can't you do anything right?" That was what his own parents had said to him when they were irritated. That is what he said to himself when he messed up. It was a natural thing to say to Frank. What else could Frank do besides feel guilty and apologize and say he would be more careful from now on? Frank does have other choices that will help him cope with cutting criticism from others.

Being in Mr. Zero's class has not been easy for Patsy. She has tried so hard to do well. Math is especially hard for her, and Mr. Zero's explanations do not make sense to her. When she asked for help at the beginning of the year, he was so sharp and sarcastic that she quit asking. Melody usually helps Patsy with math, but Patsy was not able to get together with her before the test, so she was still very confused. Mr. Zero's unjustly severe criticism was more than she could handle with all of the other frustration she was feeling. What Mr. Zero said was not true, but Patsy could not tell him that he was mistaken. She needs a way to cope with unjust and untrue criticism.

Randy's reaction to unjust criticism was quite different from Patsy's, but Randy tends to mow everyone down with his aggression no matter what the situation may be. Randy needs to learn the same things Patsy does, because he deals with unjust criticism as poorly as Patsy; however, she does not make enemies and Randy does.

Being one of the guys is very important to Kevin. He has to be rough and tough as well as hip, slick, and cool. Most of his behavior is built on looking cool. If anyone suggests that something may not be cool, Kevin will drop it fast. Since Tracy is on the football team, too, it is important to Kevin that Tracy approve of him. Tracy does not worry a lot about grades; he does just well enough to stay eligible for sports. Kevin wants to please Tracy and the guys more than he wants to please his parents. Besides, his parents will be satisfied if he gets a B; he does not need an A for anyone but himself. Mr. Hablo had encouraged Kevin to try for an A, but Kevin was not concerned with pleasing him. All the reasons for studying for the test did not carry enough weight to balance out the fact that Tracy and the guys might think less of him if he chose to stay home and study. Kevin will have difficulty developing judgment of his own and trusting that judgment if he does not learn to follow his own desires and do what is best for himself even when others might criticize his behavior.

The basic misunderstanding in every case of "criticizer" and "criticizee" is that because there is a disagreement someone must be right and someone must be wrong. It is one of our "All-American Hang-ups" and it is *not true*. If there is a disagreement, you simply disagree. No one is right and no one is wrong. If you do not do things the same way, you are different. No one is right and no one is wrong. It is okay to disagree. It is okay to be different.

You can get rid of the guilt that goes along with the implied wrong in what you do. Frank felt guilty because turning on the wrong burner was "wrong." It may have been careless, but it was not wrong. Patsy got a D and that was supposed to be "wrong." It was not wrong. That would mean that an A was "right," but then what would a C be, sort of right or sort of wrong? Not everything in the world can be handled with "right" and "wrong" labels. Coping with criticism assertively can get the labels off.

Self-criticism can be the worst kind of criticism. You may be a person who takes a little criticism from outside and turns it into a lot of criticism inside. Frank Lee does a good job of that, and Tracy beats himself every time he does something he calls "wrong." Your own self-directed criticism can be the most destructive because you will believe your Voice above all things. You must learn to talk to your critical Voice the same way you talk to critical others in your life.

Coping with Criticism

Since fear, guilt, and anxiety are your major feelings when you are criticized, you need ways of coping with criticism that will lessen those feelings. You need a variety of ways to deal with criticism that is true, untrue, or partly true and criticism that is hurtful and unjustified. Coping with criticism assertively means that you treat the other person with dignity and respect while maintaining your own sense of dignity and self-respect. You are not interested in winning or getting even or being right. You want no power struggle so there is no winning or losing, and there is room for people to be different so you do not have to be right.

Fogging

An effective technique for coping with criticism called "fogging" is described by Manuel Smith in *When I Say No, I Feel Guilty*. Fog cannot be seen through clearly, yet you can walk through it. You can throw things at it and they do not bounce. You cannot hurt fog or be hurt by it. It stays there and you cannot do anything to change it or make it go away. You finally give up trying to do anything about it.

You can learn to be a fog and handle criticism that way. People will soon give up the attack. In fogging you never agree or disagree, you never attack, you never defend. You simply fog away the criticism.

MRS. GIBE: The meeting starts at 7:30. If you weren't so lazy you'd be here.
RANDY ROARER: You might be right, Mrs. Gibe.

MR. HABLO: Kevin, you should have had an A.
KEVIN: You may be right, Mr. Hablo.
MR. HABLO: You just didn't study enough.
KEVIN: That's probably true.

CARRIE CADGER: You're awfully selfish lately.
PATSY PUSHOVER: It probably seems that way to you.

RUBY ROARER: You always take so long to eat.
MELODY MODERATE: I guess it seems so to you.
RUBY ROARER: If you don't hurry up, we'll be the last ones out.

MELODY MODERATE: You may be right. There aren't many people left.

MR. ZERO: Patsy, you're never going to learn math.
PATSY PUSHOVER: You may be right, Mr. Zero. It sure is hard for me.
MR. ZERO: If you don't do something, you're not going to pass.
PATSY PUSHOVER: That's probably true. Something must be done.

MR. LEE: Why can't you do anything right?
FRANK LEE: It must seem to you that I'm doing everything wrong lately.

Notice that the replies all contain phrases such as "It *may* seem ..., It *probably* seems ..., You *may* be ..., You're *probably* ...." Those words give agreement that fogs away what has been said. Patsy does not feel bad when Mr. Zero says she will never learn math. He *may* be right. Then again, he *may* be wrong. You do not need to be defensive when you say, "It may seem that way to you." You have neither agreed nor disagreed with the person, and you have not given up your own point of view. Fogging allows you to maintain your dignity and self-respect. You know you have insulted no one, and you feel good about yourself.

Agreeing with Criticism

At times negative criticism is justified, and you need to be able to acknowledge and accept it. Being defensive will keep the discussion going in a negative way. Agreeing with the criticism will usually stop it right there. When Ruby tells Melody that she takes too long to eat, Melody can agree with her instead of fogging. She can say, "You're right. I do like to eat slowly."

Besides ending the criticism from the other person, agreeing says that it was okay for you to do what you did. Frank did turn on the wrong burner; he can agree with the criticism. "I sure do have trouble finding the right knob on the stove, Dad. I'll have to be more careful." Tracy missed the pass, and when the coach tells him to keep his eye on the ball, Tracy can say, "You're right, Coach. I lost it this time." It is okay to make a mistake. Frank and Tracy are going to try to do better in the future. It is okay for

Melody to eat slowly if she wants to; she is not wrong. When you are late and your friend says, "You're late," do not go into a long explanation. Say, "You're right. I am late. I need to work on being on time." It will save all kinds of wear and tear thinking up excuses that no one wants to hear anyway.

Disagreeing with Criticism

Sometimes criticism is untrue and you do not want the other person to keep the wrong picture of you or to continue treating you unfairly. That is when it is appropriate to disagree with the criticism.

MR. ZERO: If you had put more effort into your homework, you would have had a better grade.
PATSY PUSHOVER: I did all of my homework, Mr. Zero, and when I missed problems I tried to find out why my answers were wrong. This chapter was very hard for me.

Patsy *had* put much effort into her homework. Mr. Zero's comment was unfair and needed to be challenged in an appropriate way.

MRS. GIBE: You're just too lazy to get up early enough to make the 7:30 committee meeting.
RANDY ROARER: I do have trouble getting up, Mrs. Gibe, but it isn't because I'm lazy. I don't get home from work until 9:30, and it is usually after 11 before my homework is done.

Randy is not lazy, and Mrs. Gibe needed to be put straight on that. Aggressiveness would make her feel justified in her opinion. The assertive response did not put her down, but it did disagree with her in an appropriate way and treated her with dignity and respect. Randy's behavior was dignified and showed his own self-respect.

CARRIE CADGER: You're awfully selfish lately.
PATSY PUSHOVER: I'm not selfish, Carrie; I don't want to lend anything.

Patsy is not going to take a negative label from Carrie. She does not need to call her names for always borrowing. Patsy's refusal to

Coping through Assertiveness

be labeled selfish is dignified. Reinforcing her earlier statement that she does not want to lend anything may not change Carrie's idea of what selfish is, but it lets Carrie know that Patsy still means what she said and will not be bullied.

> TRACY CARBON: What are you doing with that Spanish book? You don't need to study. You'll be hanging around the Dexters before long if you're not careful.
> KEVIN KOMBAT: Studying for the Spanish test isn't going to make any difference in my friends, Tracy. I'll still hang around with you even if I get a good grade.

Kevin's nondefensive disagreement does not give Tracy ammunition for anything further. The kidding comment at the end might bring, "Who said I want you hanging around?" from Tracy, but the implied criticism will have been defused.

At times only part of the criticism is true. Then you agree with the part that is true and disagree with the part that is not true.

> MR. LEE: Why can't you do anything right?
> FRANK LEE: I did turn on the wrong burner, Dad, but I usually do a good job on my chores. I don't do *everything* wrong.

> BEN EVALLENT: You're always the last one to the car.
> SAM SERVER: The past three days I've been last because I'm helping Mr. Scientific put away his insect trays. Usually I'm one of the first ones here.

> MR. ZERO: Why don't you turn your assignments in on time?
> MELODY MODERATE: I am late with this assignment, but this is only the second time all year my assignment has been late.

In each case the person has acknowledged the part of the criticism that is true and disagreed with the part that is not. It is important to be aware of your tone of voice while you are disagreeing. You need not be sharp and defensive. Make your assertive statement in a calm, firm tone of voice.

Evaluating and Asserting Yourself

You know yourself better than anyone else does. You know what you do well and what you do not do well. At times you need to assert yourself in a positive way and at other times you need to be willing to make negative assertions about yourself. If someone asks you to be in the chorus of the musical, and you do not sing well, you need to be able to say, "I don't sing well enough to be in the chorus." When you are asked to go out for the basketball team because you are well over six feet tall, you need to be able to say, "I know I'm very tall, but I don't play basketball well enough to help the team." When you hand in a paper for history and the teacher looks at the first page in dismay, you need to say, "My handwriting is not good, but I spent a lot of time on the paper. It's better than it looks. I'm taking typing next semester."

Sometimes your negative assertions open the door for further discussion. When Frank wants to ask his dad for the car, a negative assertion will take away some of his dad's resistance. "Dad, I've done some really stupid things lately, but I am trying to do better." Frank's dad can respond either positively or negatively, but this beginning gives Frank a chance to tell about some of the more positive things that he has done. Tracy can tell the coach, "I'm having a hard time holding on to the ball lately, Coach. I feel real bad about that." He is likely to receive help rather than more criticism.

When you admit your weaknesses, other people do not seem to have as much of a need to point them out for you. Equally important for you, however, is to be able to admit your strong points as well. There are times when you need to let other people know the things that you do well. When Ben Evallent wants to make some extra money and he hears Mr. Neighbor say how badly his car needs washing and waxing, Ben needs to speak up and say, "I do a good job washing and waxing cars, Mr. Neighbor. My price is very reasonable, and I do the inside, too." If Torey Nato wants to get more involved in school activities, she needs to be able to say to the drama teacher, "I paint scenery very well. I worked on scenery at my other school for the past two years." During a job interview when you are asked if you are a good typist and you are, you need to reply, "Yes, I type fast and accurately." Evaluating your strengths and asserting them gives people necessary information about you. Be aware that your Voice will have some negative comments about your positive assertions. The Voice will tell you that you are bragging or that you should not tell others how good you are. Remind the Voice that you do type well or sing well or write well or that you do have the skills for the job.

Evaluating your strengths and weaknesses helps you to decide

whether to accept or reject criticism. When Carrie called Patsy
selfish, Patsy was able to reject the criticism because she had
evaluated her motives and knew she was not refusing Carrie's
requests to borrow things out of selfishness. Frank Lee admitted
that he had turned on the wrong burner, but he rejected the idea
that he never did anything right. He made the positive assertion
that he had done a good job on his chores. Judging yourself fairly
and accurately takes practice and often means quieting the Voice
that wants you to believe the negative things without giving you
credit for the positive.

Delaying

It would be nice if you always knew what to say in every
situation, but that is not life. There will be times when you are
completely at a loss, and the criticism leaves you feeling confused
and uncertain. The assertive thing to do is to admit it and say you
would like to give it some thought. Pamela Butler in *Self-Assertion
for Women* calls this "delaying." Rather than being defensive or
feeling totally unable to cope, you can say, "I'm not sure how I
feel about that. I'd like to think about it for a while," or "I feel
confused about that, and I can't talk about it right now," or "I'd
like to think about that and talk about it later."

When you have used a delaying tactic, it is important that you
do talk about the subject later. Do not allow it to go by without
bringing it up later. You need the time to sort out your feelings
and reactions to what has been said. Taking the extra time allows
you to respond in a more appropriate way. The tendency to react
defensively or let it go completely can be overcome by having an
assertive delaying sentence ready. "I'd like to think about that for
a few minutes." Then after you have thought about it, open the
subject again by saying, "I've had time to think about what you
said, and I can agree with ...," or "I've thought about what you
said, and I disagree with ...." Do not think that you miss your
chance when you cannot think of an immediate reply. It is never
too late to be assertive, and delaying can allow you time to frame a
good assertive response.

Coping with Compliments

With so much concern about how to cope with criticism, you
would think that coping with compliments would be easy. Not so.
For most people, handling compliments is just as difficult as

dealing with criticism. Compliments may make you feel uncomfortable. You do not know what to say. Your hands and feet suddenly become huge, and your face feels on fire. Positive regard from others is important, but when you get it, you do not know what to do with it.

Patsy Pushover responds to compliments by blushing and looking at the floor. When Penny says that she likes Ruby's skirt, Ruby says, "This old thing? I've had it since junior high." Kevin does not know how to react so he looks stony-faced when Mrs. Literate tells him that the story he wrote for English is the most entertaining one she has read all year. Coping with compliments can be a problem.

When you do not know what to say, you can always say, "Thank you." It works every time. "Thank you" acknowledges that you have heard and received what was said and appreciate it. There are appropriate things you can add. Kevin worked hard on his story, so a good reply for him is, "Thank you. I'm glad you like it. I enjoyed writing it and worked hard on it." Ruby's reply could be, "Thank you. It's been one of my favorite skirts for a long time." The self-assertion along with the thank you is an added acknowledgment that what the person said mattered to you. It also says to you that you have shown good judgment or are proud of your accomplishments. Ruby made a good choice of clothing, and Kevin did a good job on his story. The positive assertion beginning with "I" gives your response that little something extra. Some assertions you can use for replying to compliments are: "I'm so glad you noticed." "I'm glad you like it." "It's one of my favorites." "I like it very much, too." "I feel good about it, too." "I spent a lot of time on it." "I'm glad you told me." "I worked hard on it." "I think I did a good job, too."

Even though you are your own judge, the positive regard of others feels good. Let them know that you appreciate their compliments.

CHAPTER VIII

Coping with Parents Assertively

Ruby Roarer was watching her favorite TV program when her mother came into the room.

MOTHER: Ruby, you didn't take the garbage out after dinner.
RUBY: I'll take it out when this program is over.
MOTHER: You take it out right now.
RUBY: Why do you always think about garbage in the middle of a program?
MOTHER: Don't get smart, young lady. Get in there and take out that garbage.
RUBY: I'll take it out during the next commercial.
MOTHER: You'll take it out now.
RUBY: If it's so important, why don't you take it out yourself?
MOTHER: Don't you talk to me like that!
RUBY: Well, what do you expect when you come in here and make such a big deal out of stupid garbage.
MOTHER: You get that garbage out and then go to your room!

Tracy Carbon was lying on the floor in the living room listening to the stereo when his mother came in.

MOTHER: Your room is a mess. Nothing is hung up or put away. Your clothes are thrown all over the place. It's impossible to tell the clean ones from the dirty ones.
TRACY: I know which ones are which.
MOTHER: Don't get smart with me. That room is a mess and it better be cleaned up.
TRACY: Whatever.
MOTHER: Don't whatever me. I want it cleaned up.
TRACY: All right. I heard you.
MOTHER: Don't talk to me in that tone of voice. You get in there right now and get that room cleaned!
TRACY: I said all right.
MOTHER: Don't say another word. Just go.

TRACY: All right, I'm going.
MOTHER: Not another word.
TRACY: All right.

Penny Passive was sitting at the dining-room table with her books out to do her homework. Her father came in:

DAD: Penny, you promised to play Yahtzee with the little ones tonight.
PENNY: Yeah, but I have so much homework to do, I can't.
DAD: You could play just a little while so we could have some peace and quiet around here.
PENNY: Yeah, but if I do, Dad, I won't get my math done, and Mr. Zero will get mad.
DAD: Your math should be done by now. Your mother let you out of helping with the dishes because you said you had math to do. Were you on the phone?
PENNY: Yeah, but I had to call Torey because we have a big problem with the scenery for the play. We had to talk about it tonight.
DAD: You know you are not to talk on the phone when you have homework or chores to do.
PENNY: Yeah, but this was *really* important, Dad.
DAD: Penny, you are absolutely exasperating. You always have some important reason why you can't do what you're supposed to or why you're doing what you're not supposed to.

Sam Server has been wanting to get his driver's license for two months now. He has done everything that is legally required to get the license, and all he needs is his father's signature on the papers.

SAM: Dad, will you sign the papers so I can get my driver's license?
DAD: We've been through this before, Sam. You have to show me the money for the insurance before I'll sign the papers.
SAM: Dad, I'll have the money to make the payment every month, I promise.
DAD: I want the whole year's worth up front.
SAM: Nobody else's parents make them pay for the whole year. Why do you always make things hard for me?
DAD: I don't care what everybody else's parents do. Don't give me that stuff. I'm not trying to make things hard for you,

I'm trying to protect myself.

SAM: (Sarcastically.) Oh, sure, you're protecting yourself. You're just afraid that you might have to put out ten cents for me. You never do anything for me.

DAD: You ungrateful little punk! I never do anything for you? See how long it takes to get those papers signed.

SAM: You're just a jerk.

What is happening? Everyone is in a roaring battle with parents within a few minutes. How do you cope with such unreasonable parents? Parents are always ragging on young people and do not even try to get along. How can you cope with such people assertively? It is possible, but you never will cope assertively until you take responsibility for your relationship with your parents. If you are unhappy or dissatisfied with the way things are at home, if you do not like the way you are being treated, take a look at yourself and decide what you can do to make it better. Do not expect your parents to change to make things better for you. If you want more respect from your parents, if you want them to listen to you and take you seriously, you must decide that *you will get along with them*. That means that you must look at what is happening and ask, "What am I doing that is bringing this negative reaction from my parents?" Then you must determine how you can use what you have learned about assertiveness to change the negative reaction to positive.

Focus on Yourself Rather Than on Parents

To begin with, you need to keep centered on yourself. Keep the responsibility for your behavior on yourself. You are responsible for your world, and the problems in your life are *your* problems. Though it seems that your parents are responsible for creating situations that cause you trouble, how you deal with those situations determines what your life is like. How you think about what is happening determines how you cope with it. Sam could certainly say that his father is unreasonable. Ruby's mother sure is irritating, and Tracy's mother seems to get excited over a word or two. Parents certainly have problems getting along with young people. If that is the way you are looking at the problem, you will never cope effectively with your parents.

Stop putting the problems on parents. Instead, begin to think, "Sam has a problem with his dad. Ruby has a problem with her mom. I have a problem with my dad. I have a problem with my mother." Once you own (accept responsibility for) the problem, you can begin to do something about it. As long as your dad has the problem, you cannot do anything to help yourself, and it is *you* that you want to help, not your parents.

Now that you are willing to admit that you have a problem and to look at yourself as responsible for it, you need to know some basic things about how you are presently dealing with other people. No matter how confused you may feel, no matter how effective or ineffective you may be, no matter how you are getting along with others, you are always doing the best you can. You always do the best you can with what you know at the time. The fact that you are reading this indicates that you want to learn more so you can do better. Give yourself a pat on the back and get ready for the changes you are going to make as "the best you can" gets better through assertiveness.

Cope with Dignity and Respect

The most important thing you have learned about assertiveness is that it is a way to treat yourself and others with dignity and respect. Ruby, Tracy, and Sam were not treated with dignity and respect. They did not treat their parents with dignity and respect, either. You may feel that since they were treated disrespectfully, they had every right to be disrespectful in return. You will never be treated respectfully yourself as long as you treat others disrespectfully. You will never be treated with dignity until you behave with dignity. You do not need to wait for respect from others before being respectful to yourself. It is your responsibility to treat yourself with dignity and respect. To do that, you have to treat others with dignity and respect regardless of how they treat you. However, you will find that when you behave in a dignified manner and are respectful toward others and yourself, you will receive respect from others.

Accept Humanness of Parents

When you were very small, you considered your parents omnipotent, all-powerful. They knew *everything*. They were always right. As a teenager your attitude surely changed, and many parents feel that, in your eyes, they can do *nothing* right. This change in attitude comes about gradually and is perfectly normal unless it is extreme. As you grow and learn about people, you begin to realize that parents are not always right. They make good decisions and bad decisions. In fact, they are real honest-to-goodness human beings. Being human means making mistakes now and then.

For some reason, you continue to expect your parents to be perfect. You expect them always to make good decisions. You expect them to do what you think good parents *should* do. When they don't, you feel let down and angry. Young people spend a lot of time screaming, "It's not fair!" Who said life was fair? Young people do a lot of judging that gets them nowhere. All the times you have said, "Fathers are supposed to ... Everyone else's mother ... Parents shouldn't ..." have done nothing toward dealing with your problems. It doesn't matter what you think fathers are supposed to do, what everyone else's mother does, or what parents should or shouldn't do. You have the situation as it is.

Expecting other people to change will cause you no end of grief. Expecting other people to do what "should" be done will leave you frustrated and unhappy. A willingness to accept adults as they are and make decisions about your behavior that help you get along with other human beings will open doors to new and better relationships with parents. Just as you want to be given the right to make mistakes, give adults a chance when they make mistakes. Do not condemn too harshly. They do the best they can. Instead, take the responsibility for improving your relationships with the adults in your life.

Accept the Hierarchy of Authority

Parents are always giving orders, and young people are supposed to jump up and do everything when their parents want it done. Tracy's mother wanted his room cleaned up right now. Ruby's mother wanted the garbage out right now. Why must everything be done when parents want it done? Why was it so "smart" for Ruby to ask her mother, "Why do you always think about garbage in the middle of a program?" What made her mother fly into a rage over, "If it's so important, why don't you take it out yourself?" Ruby broke an important rule. It is an unspoken rule, for the most part, but you are supposed to know it. It is the rule that "This is the way young people are *supposed* to behave." Unfortunately, different adults see what is *supposed* to

be right differently. They have different ways that you are
supposed to behave. However, all agree on the basic principle of
why you are *supposed* to behave the way they expect you to. The
best way to explain the how and the why is with some examples.

One day Sergeant Barksalot was giving the orders of the day to
his men. The scene went something like this:

SERGEANT BARKSALOT: Private Swift, latrine duty.
PRIVATE SWIFT: I don't want to clean toilets.
SERGEANT BARKSALOT: Latrine duty, Swift.
PRIVATE SWIFT: No way am I going to clean toilets. You
better give me something else to do. I'm not cleaning toilets.

Private Swift does not seem to understand that Sergeant Barksalot
has more rank and that makes his word law. Such insubordination
would get Swift into deep trouble, fast!

Imagine the following scene between Mr. Complicated of the
Complicated Computer Company and Mr. Employee.

MR. COMPLICATED: Employee, this order has to be completed today.
MR. EMPLOYEE: I don't feel too well today. I'll do it
tomorrow.
MR. COMPLICATED: This has to be done right now.
MR. EMPLOYEE: You always make a big deal about everything. I'll finish it tomorrow.

It is not at all complicated to see that Mr. Employee is on his way
to being Mr. Ex-Employee.

Armies and businesses cannot accomplish their purposes unless
there are those who give orders and those who follow orders. Look
around and you will see that the world is orderly and systematic.
All around us nature demonstrates an orderly system. Human
beings as part of nature require order also. No matter what society
or culture you visit, you will find systems that keep the culture
operating in some orderly way. Systems may be very different
from each other, but there is always some kind of order. Within
each society there are rules for government, education, employ-
ment, and all areas of life. Every system in the society has a
hierarchy. A hierarchy is a system of ranking things—Sergeant
Barksalot above Private Swift, Mr. Complicated above Mr. Employee.

You are part of a hierarchy in society, in your family, at school, and in any group of which you are a member. In all societies, the older, more mature members are in positions of authority over the younger, less mature. That is true in the animal kingdom as well. Until the young reach adulthood, they do not have equality with adults in the hierarchy. It is a fact of life that young people are on a lower rung of the hierarchical ladder than adults. Some young people do not like to accept that fact and consider it very unfair. Whether you like it or not, however, young people and adults are not equal. Ruby's mother did not like being told to take the garbage out herself because young people are not *supposed* to speak to older people disrespectfully. Young people are *supposed* to do what they are told to do when they are told to do it. When young people behave in a way they are not *supposed* to, it is because they are not in place on the hierarchical ladder. That causes a major disturbance in the way things are *supposed* to be. If you do not accept the fact that adults and children are not equal in the hierarchy, you can get so involved in fighting the system that you never look at your opportunities for using the system to your own advantage.

Do not worry about losing your rights as a human being or always having to give in because adults make decisions or demands. It is important that you have your needs met and that the adults in your life meet their needs, too. Think of an adult's wishes as a wall in front of you. You can rage and kick at the wall, but it will not move, and you cannot get by it. You hurt yourself when you kick it. If you blast a hole in it, you can get beyond it, but you have destroyed the wall. Using force and head-on confrontation is not very productive. If you cannot get through the wall, doesn't it make sense to accept the fact of the wall and to find a way around it or build a gate through it?

When you run into a wall of parental decisions that you disagree with, a head-on confrontation usually hurts you. If you do manage to blast through, your parents have been hurt, their dignity has been destroyed. You are hurt along with them because destroying their dignity has required the destruction of your own. Stop kicking the wall and put that energy to work learning to assertively build a gate through it.

Some things that you do build a wall rather than a gate. They irritate people in general, but when young people do them to parents, the reaction is instantaneous fury. You need to stop doing five things:

1. Talking back.
2. Trying to get the last word.
3. Saying Yabbut.
4. Using prefaces.
5. Labeling, name-calling, and sarcasm.

Talking back, saying Yabbut, and labeling, name-calling, and sarcasm are ways young people often react to adults. You cannot just stop the back talk or sarcasm without having some way to let your feelings be known. By being assertive rather than aggressive, you can express your feelings, maintain your dignity, and be so respectful that adults will have to look at their behavior instead of yours.

Stop Talking Back

Back talk is epidemic. In every TV sit-com with children, there is always some little darling who has a swift retort for everything. It may be funny on TV, but those cutesy comebacks are actually disrespectful back talk to adults. When adults say or do things that make you angry or put you down, it is difficult to hold back that disrespectful, biting remark. "If it's so important, why don't you take it out yourself?" and "Well, what do you expect when you come in here and make such a big deal over stupid garbage?" are examples of back talk showing that Ruby did not accept the hierarchy in society. She did not recognize the fact that talking back to adults is disrespectful. She has not accepted her position in the hierarchy and is still kicking at the wall.

Young people often do not realize that the way they talk to their friends is not an acceptable way to talk to adults. The swift comebacks become disrespectful back talk from a young person to an adult. Two adults may say things to each other that are taken in fun because of the equal relationship. The same thing said by a young person to an adult becomes disrespectful back talk.

Back talk generally starts an argument and leads to anger and resentment for everyone. It is a great exercise in wall kicking and wondering why your toe hurts. You may feel enraged over your treatment by the adult, but talking back only makes matters worse. You need to find something else to do rather than lashing out with back talk. You need to put that energy to work in a positive, assertive way of expressing your feelings.

Stop Trying to Get the Last Word

Getting the last word is a game that young people and parents play and often do not know they are playing. Some people mistake it for back talk, but it is a different game. Tracy played the game very well with his mother. "All right" said one more time can keep the conflict going, and Tracy had to make one more remark after his mother stopped talking. It is infuriating to adults and can escalate into all-out war unless someone stops the game. Why not take the responsibility and give your parents the last word? Tell yourself that you are doing it for the sake of peace in *your* world. It will cut down on your aggravation. You will not have to listen to adults go on forever. Your comments just keep things moving; when you stop, the adults will, too.

Stop Saying Yabbut

Yabbut is the favorite expression of the person who does not want to do something. Penny had a Yabbut for everything her father wanted her to do and for doing what she knew she was not supposed to do. "Yeah, but I have so much homework I can't." "Yeah, but if I do I won't get my math done." "Yeah, but I had to talk to Torey."

When you say Yabbut (Yeah, but), you tell people that what they want is not important to you; what they expect you are not willing to give them. You tell them that their thoughts and opinions are not of interest to you.

Try to catch yourself before you say Yabbut. Listen to others and become aware of how many times they use it to duck a responsibility or a job. Become aware of how you feel when you make a suggestion or a request and someone says Yabbut to you. It may explain why you feel angry.

Especially irritating to adults is having a "minilecture" interrupted with Yabbut. When the lecture starts you really do not want to listen to it, you have heard it a hundred times, and the adult does not understand how things are nowadays. However, being interrupted with "Yabbut things are different now and everybody else gets to ..." sends an adult into orbit. You might just as well say, "You don't know what you're talking about. I know what's going on and you don't." Being assertive means taking Yabbut out of your vocabulary.

Stop Using Prefacing Statements and Questions

You have seen prefaces at the beginning of books. You may not be aware that you are introducing some of what you say with prefaces. In verbal interactions, there are questions and statements that everyone—young, old, or in between—uses to preface what is said. Most of the questions and statements serve as triggers for firing the first shot in the battle. They certainly did in Sam's case: "Nobody else's parents make them pay for a whole year." "Why do you always make things hard for me?" "How come you never do anything for me?" When Sam threw those in, his father got hostile.

Questions that serve to trigger anger are not meant to be answered but often provoke a sarcastic, angry response.

Why do you always...?
Why can't I ever...?
How many times do I have to tell you...?
Why do I always have to...?
How come you never...?
Don't you ever listen...?
Why can't you be like...?

Some statements create an immediate start to hostilities:

I've told you a hundred times...
You never let me...
Everybody else's mother/father...
You always let him...
Nobody else has to...
You should/shouldn't...
You have no right to...
I know you're going to get mad...
I know you're going to say no...

Do you really want an answer to "Why can't I ever," or do you want an argument? Usually, "Why can't I ever," means this is the second time you could not, and you want to argue your parents into letting you do whatever it is. Parents then feel defensive, and most feel that they have to justify their decision. They begin explaining, and you counter everything with further arguments from your point of view, and the battle is on. So much energy used for so little good. The anger and resentment are not worth it.

Most of the time prefaces are automatic, and you do not even know you are using them until they are out of your mouth. Everyone says them. Just listen. Also, listen to your inner response when an adult uses them on you. "How many times do I have to tell you ..." makes you want to scream, "4,892!"

Rather than opening up discussion, preface statements close it off. A statement that begins, "You should ..." tells the other person that you have judged her/his behavior, and it was not acceptable to you. An immediate response to "You should ..." is "I won't." Another favorite of young people is, "I know you'll say no ..." Since you have already read the adult's mind and know the answer, there is no need to go any further. You are absolutely right, the answer is no. Preface statements trigger immediate anger. There is no discussion from that point; it is all-out war!

Preface statements and questions serve no useful purpose. You hate it when adults use them on you. Take a lesson from them and get rid of the preface statements and questions and the irritation that goes with them.

Stop Labeling, Name-Calling, and Sarcasm

Labeling and name-calling are felt deeply and resented bitterly by young people. No one likes to be called a jerk or a punk or worse. No one likes to be labeled lazy, trouble-maker, or stupid. In fact, when the name-calling starts, the fight is not far behind.

In some families there is a lot of name-calling. Sometimes it is done by the parents. That does not make it okay. If your parents do call you names—and it hurts deeply if they do—do not retaliate in kind. When you call them names, it only adds fuel to the fire of their anger, and believe it or not, they are hurt, too.

When Sam's dad called him a punk, it hurt Sam, and he called his dad a jerk. That kind of name-calling makes everyone feel miserable. The fact that his father had hurt him did not make it okay for Sam to hurt back. Aside from the disrespect to his father, it was disrespectful to Sam himself. Where was his dignity when he called his father a jerk? As a person, you think more of yourself than to get into name-calling with an adult or anyone else. You have more dignity than to stoop to that. The self-respecting person you are does not call other people names. Keep in mind how important your dignity and self-respect are to you.

Cutting sarcasm does just that—it cuts deeply and leaves you wounded and hurting. So often with sarcasm, it is not what is said but how it is said that does the damage. Young people complain about adult sarcasm more than anything else, but it is no less cutting or hurtful when you are sarcastic to adults. You may have had a good model for sharpening your tongue, and it may be difficult to keep from returning the sarcastic remarks. However, keep in mind that your dignity and respect for yourself allow you to give others more dignity and respect than they may give themselves.

Let your dislike of being called names and being the brunt of sarcastic comments help you avoid giving that same hurt to others. There is a better way to deal with sarcasm than returning the favor. You can express your feelings in an appropriate, assertive way.

Responding to Parents' Demands

The aggressive responses of Ruby, Sam, Tracy, and Penny made their parents frustrated and angry and got the young people in more trouble. Aggressiveness does not pay off. But if all you do is stop being aggressive, you will become frustrated and resentful because, as you know, passiveness is also a no-win situation.

Assertiveness is expressing your feelings honestly, directly, and appropriately in a way that does not violate the rights of others. Ruby, Sam, Tracy, and Penny did not express their feelings at all. They gave aggressive responses that made things worse. Assertive responses take the heat out of exchanges with parents. Here is a replay of Ruby, using assertiveness:

MOTHER: Ruby, you didn't take the garbage out after dinner.
RUBY: You're right, Mom, I didn't.
MOTHER: Well, when are you going to do it?
RUBY: I'll do it during the next commercial.
MOTHER: Don't you forget.

Ruby's mother was all ready for a big fuss, but when Ruby agreed with her, the argument ended. Ruby had a chance to say when she would do it what her mother wanted, so she did not feel resentful about having to do it.

Agreeing with the truth is a good technique for Tracy to use when his mother tells him about the mess in his room. The conversation has to go in a different direction when Tracy agrees.

TRACY: You're right, Mom, my room is a mess.
MOM: Are you getting smart with me?
TRACY: No, Mom, I'm serious. I know my room is a mess.
MOM: Only a filthy slob would have a room like that. I want it cleaned up right now.

Tracy has agreed with the truth, but his mother has called him a filthy slob, and he is not happy at all. The most natural response for Tracy is an aggressive, "It's not your room. I don't see why you want to make such a big deal out of it. Nobody could keep a room as perfect as you want it!" Tracy is dancing all around what is really bothering him. He is not looking at what he is feeling about being called a filthy slob, even though that is what he is reacting to. In dealing with this assertively, Tracy must express his feelings appropriately. Underneath the anger that comes to him immediately, what is he feeling? Tracy feels hurt about being called a filthy slob. He needs to share those feelings with his mother in an "I" statement.

TRACY: I feel hurt when I'm called a filthy slob. I know my room is a mess, but when I'm called a filthy slob, I don't want to clean it up.
MOTHER: Well, that's just too bad. I want that room cleaned up whether you want to do it or not.
TRACY: I'll do my room, Mom, but I really feel hurt about being called a slob.
MOTHER: If the room were clean, I wouldn't call you a slob.

Tracy has focused on his feelings, and his assertive "I" statement does not bring out defensive feelings or resentment from his mother. She got the last word, but that is okay. Tracy has owned his feelings and is in control of himself. He has not put his mother down, has not been disrespectful, but he has focused on the real issue that hurt him. His mother is left to consider the fact that Tracy feels hurt about being called a slob. An aggressive response would have left his mother angry about *his* disrespectful behavior toward *her*. Now she is focused on *her* disrespectful behavior toward *him*. A calm, assertive "I" statement has positive power for expressing feelings appropriately.

Penny is nonassertive and passive. She has difficulty saying no or disagreeing with anyone. Penny would never talk back. She is always very slow or does not get around to things. She agrees to anything and then does not follow through. Her parents get very frustrated, but Penny is always respectful and never argues, so they feel guilty about being so infuriated when she does not get things done.

Penny does not know that her passiveness is indirectly very aggressive. It is sneaky because she does not openly defy anyone. She quietly does what she wants to do and ignores the wishes of others. She forgets or has so much to do that she cannot get around to doing what other people want. She always has a good reason for not doing what was expected. Penny's Yabbuts tell others that she does not think their wants and needs are important. Her need to express her feelings honestly, directly, and appropriately is equal to the need of other very aggressive people to express their feelings appropriately.

Since Penny does not keep her commitments, she must learn to agree with the truth when her father confronts her. She also must become aware of what she is feeling and express her feelings directly so that she will stop her passive aggression and begin to make commitments that she will keep.

> FATHER: Penny, you promised to play Yahtzee with the little ones tonight.
> PENNY: You're right. I did say I would.
> FATHER: They said you told them you were too busy.
> PENNY: I did tell them that, Dad.
> FATHER: They're really disappointed and want me to make you play with them.
> PENNY: I feel bad about putting you in a spot like that, but I really don't want to play with them tonight, and I do have a lot of homework.
> FATHER: I know they get on your nerves, Penny, but it's a big deal when you play with them.
> PENNY: I know how much they like it, but I really don't want to play tonight. I'll play with them another night, but you know how it is when you just don't want to do something.
> FATHER: Well, if you feel that negative about playing tonight, I'll tell them you'll play another time. I expect you to tell them when you'll play and be sure that you do.
> PENNY: Thanks, Dad. I'll talk to them before they go to bed.

Penny's direct honesty about her feelings keeps the conversation focused on how she feels about playing with her little brother and sister tonight. Her father may not be that reasonable, or he may try to make her feel guilty so she will play. He might even say that he does not care whether she wants to play or not, she promised and he expects her to do so. In that case, Penny can say, "If you think it's that important, I'll play tonight." Because she expressed her feelings and her dad knows how she feels, Penny can play Yahtzee and not carry resentment about being held to her agreement. Her assertiveness has made it possible for her to evaluate the situation and decide that even though she would rather not play, she would feel better about the situation if she did play. She does not feel that she "should" play; she has chosen and is willing to play.

Assertiveness gives you a choice. Ruby does not *want* to take the garbage out but now *is willing* to. Tracy does not *want* to clean his room, but now he *is willing* to do it. Expressing your feelings honestly and directly allows you to feel willing to consider the needs of others.

Coping with Parents' Criticism

Parents can be extremely critical and see only the bad, not giving you credit for the good. The usual response to criticism of this kind is, "You make me so mad. You never give me credit for what I do right." Such an accusing response puts parents on the defensive, and they become angry at being challenged. "You make me so mad" implies that your parent is responsible for your feelings. It blames your parent for how you feel. Not enjoying being blamed, your parent will let you know how *you* make *her* angry. "You never give me credit" is also blaming and accusing. Your parent feels that he must justify his behavior, and that makes him feel angry and resentful. To avoid angry confrontations, use assertiveness when responding to unjust criticism.

MOTHER: This room is always a mess.
TRACY: It's pretty messy today, but I've had it in good shape for the past four days.

MOTHER: You're so careless. You're always getting something all over the floor.
RUBY: It may have looked careless, but I was being careful. This is the first thing I've spilled since the tomato soup last winter. Cleaning that up made me want to be careful!

FATHER: You left the socket wrenches out. Why don't you ever put things away?
KEVIN: I may leave things around sometimes, Dad, but this is the first time I've left tools out.

FATHER: You were supposed to do the yard today. You can't expect to be paid for a half-way job. You didn't even do the edging.
RANDY: I can see why you might think that, but I'm not finished yet. I did a good job on the yard. I got all the weeding done and the grass cut and raked. I plan to do the edging and sweep the sidewalk after dinner. Then I want you to inspect the job before you pay me.

MOTHER: The stove isn't clean. I told you to clean the kitchen.
TOREY: You're right, I didn't clean the stove, but I did clean the kitchen. All the food is put away, the dishes are done, and the sink and drainboard are clean.

You know the kinds of things you are regularly criticized for. You can think about the situations ahead of time and decide how you will cope with them the next time they occur. You have several choices. Ruby and Randy did some fogging with "It may have looked careless" and "I can see why you might think that." Tracy and Torey agreed with the truth in the criticism and then made their positive assertions. Kevin made a straight assertion of his usual behavior regarding tools. Choose the assertive strategy that best fits your situation. Practice what you are going to say so that when the situation comes up, you will be able to cope with it assertively.

Opening Positive Discussion

Sam wants his driver's license very badly. He and his father have gone over the issue time and time again. Before he started, Sam knew where the discussion was going to go but was hoping that his father would react differently this time. Sam is the one who has to do things differently. There is a Three-Step Plan that will allow Sam to get his needs met by assertively opening positive discussion: Step 1. Own the problem and ask for help. Step 2. Offer alternatives. Step 3. Be willing to negotiate.

Step 1. *Own the problem and ask for help.*

SAM: Dad, I have a problem, and I'd like your help.

DAD: (Overjoyed because Sam is coming to him with a problem and wants to confide in him.) I'll help if I can. What can I do?

SAM: It's about my driver's license. I know how important it is to you to have me covered by insurance, and it's only fair for me to pay my share of the insurance.

DAD: You want me to change my mind about having the first year's money up front.

SAM: Wait a second, Dad. I'm not asking you to change your mind.

DAD: Then what do you want?

Step 2. *Offer alternatives.*

SAM: I've been saving for five months now, and I have enough to pay the first six months' insurance. I think that shows I'm committed to paying the insurance.

DAD: That's true, Sam. I'm proud of the way you've saved so far.

SAM: Well, then, Dad, could I pay for six months' insurance now with the agreement that at the end of six months I'll give you the money for the last six months?

DAD: Oh, I don't know about that, Sam.

SAM: I know it's a lot of money to lend me, but I've saved that amount in just five months. I know I could have the rest for you in another six months.

DAD: Well, I don't know. Six months is a long time for me to wait and then find out you're short some of the money.

Step 3. *Be willing to negotiate.*

SAM: I could give you some money every month.

DAD: I don't want to bother with that. We've talked about that before.

SAM: How about if I gave you half of what I'd owe after three months and the rest after another three months?

DAD: Well, I'm not sure.

SAM: If I pay you half now and the other half in three-month installments, I'll have the rest of the year to save for next year's insurance.

DAD: You know, Sam, you sound like you've really thought this out. You *have* been conscientious about saving. I think I'm

willing to go along with you.
SAM: All right! Thanks, Dad. Then you'll sign for my license?
DAD: You bet, Son. Get the papers.

Sam felt that he was being treated unfairly by his father, so he needed a way to discuss the problem without getting into an argument. The Three-Step Plan kept Sam focused on himself the whole time. He did not complain to his dad; he offered an alternative and had a few others in reserve. Sam kept responsibility for working out the compromise. He pointed out what he had already accomplished with a positive assertion about his commitment to saving. Sam's assertiveness and use of the Three-Step Plan were very effective.

Rita Booker has a recurring problem and would use the Three-Step Plan like this:

Step 1.   *Own the problem and ask for help.*
RITA: Mom, I have a problem and I'd like your help.
MOM: Well, I'll help if I can. What is it?
RITA: I may be making a big thing out of nothing, but I'm really upset about having to do the dishes for Bill again tonight. He leaves as soon as he finishes eating, even when it's his turn to do the dishes. I'd like your help in figuring out a fair way to handle this.
MOM: Well, I'll remind him tomorrow. Sometimes it's hard to get him to do his jobs. (Rita know this will not work, so she moves to Step 2.)

Step 2.   *Offer alternatives.*
RITA: I have an idea for something we might do. Bill and I are supposed to take turns doing all the jobs around the house. There are some jobs that I'm willing to do all the time if Bill will do some of the others all the time.
MOM: That sounds good to me, but we'll have to talk to Bill about it.

Step 3.   *Be willing to negotiate.*
RITA: I'm willing to sit down with you and Bill and work something out. When we decide on which jobs each of us will do, I think it would be fair if you and Dad agree that I won't have to do Bill's jobs if he doesn't do them as long as I've done all of my jobs. (It is important for Rita to establish the fairness

of the agreement. Later, if Bill does not do his jobs, her parents will have to agree to the fairness of her not having to do his jobs.)

MOM: I'll talk to Dad about it.

RITA: Thanks, Mom, I knew I could count on you to help.

Later, after parents, Rita, and Bill have discussed the matter:

MOM: The garbage needs to be taken out.

RITA: That's Bill's job, Mom. We agreed that it would be fair for Bill to be responsible for all of his jobs if I'm responsible about doing all of mine. (This can be said only if Rita has indeed been responsible about doing all of her jobs. She must be sure to cover herself on this one!)

Using the car is often a big issue for parents and young people. You can negotiate assertively for car privileges.

YOU: Dad, I have a problem and I think you can help me with it. I always seem to be arguing about using the car (this is "owning" the problem of arguing about using the car and not accusing Dad of being unreasonable), and I'd like to work out an agreement with you. I know you want me to earn the right to use it, so I've come up with some guidelines. (These are your alternatives and can be in any form that works into your family's way of doing things.)

YOU (continued): I agree to do my jobs around the house. (These should be listed.) If I've done the things I'm supposed to do, then I'll be allowed to use the car either Friday or Saturday, and I will have it home by 1:00 a.m. One night each week I'll be allowed to use the car and I'll be home by 9:30. If I don't keep my part of the bargain, I lose car privileges for that week.

At this point, be willing to negotiate (not argue to get everything you want) the specific jobs or behavior that your parents want; for example, no grumbling about doing your jobs; no fighting with your sister/brother; the garbage taken out immediately after dinner every night.

When you are willing to accept responsibility for the problem, adults are much more willing to discuss it with you. If you feel a parent has been unjust or unfair, the Three-Step Plan can work for you. Be sure you are calm and that your feelings of injustice are not influenced by your anger. By not accusing your parents of unfairness but owning the problem yourself, you make it possible to discuss a situation, not argue about it. You can give a little because you are not defending a position. Your parents can give a little because they do not feel threatened or defensive. There is a true possibility for positive discussion and agreement. Coping with parents assertively is treating them and yourself with dignity and respect.

In any situation, how well you have dealt with your parents can be measured by how good you feel about yourself. When you argue with your parents and treat them disrespectfully, you do not feel good about what happened or about yourself. You may feel justified in your behavior, but you do not feel good about yourself. Being assertive helps you build self-esteem because you feel good about getting along better with your parents. You feel good about standing up for your rights without intruding on the rights of others. You have a sense of dignity and well-being because you have treated yourself with respect.

CHAPTER IX

Coping with Other Adults

Kay Kind answered the phone and took care of the appointment book in a beauty salon after school and on Saturdays. The owner of the shop, Harriet Cutter, was a good friend of Kay's mother and had known Kay since she was born. Kay had always liked her "Aunt" Harrie and was enjoying her job at the shop, but she was uncomfortable about the inconsistent way she was being paid. When Kay was hired seven weeks before, it was agreed that she would be paid every two weeks. The first pay period Harrie paid Kay two days late. The second pay period she paid Kay four days late, saying it had slipped her mind. It was now over a week since Kay should have been paid, and Harrie still had not paid her. Kay needed the money, but she did not know how to ask Harrie to pay her and felt embarrassed about asking.

Fred Friendly had always been close to his grandparents. They were very special to him, but lately it had become painful being around them. Fred had let his hair grow a little so that it covered his ears and was just short of his collar. Several of his friends, boys and girls, had mentioned how much they liked it, and Fred felt that it really looked good. That is, he felt it looked good until he was around his grandfather. Then Fred's hair became a symbol of everything his grandfather disliked in American youth today. Fred was beginning to avoid going to see his grandparents and tried to be absent when they came to visit. When his dad noticed his withdrawal, Fred was able to tell his dad how his grandfather's constant criticism was affecting him. Fred's dad advised him to explain his feelings to his grandfather, because Grandfather was beginning to feel rejected. Fred did want to tell his grandfather to get off his case, but he did not know how to do it without being offensive.

Scott Scoffer was sitting in the office of the Dean of Boys because of Mr. Zero. "He is such a jerk," thought Scott. "He had no right to call me stupid in front of the class. He deserved what I said to him, and I'll tell him off again if he puts me down like that."

The composition papers have just been handed back and Sally Simmer has a C. She looks through the five pages of work to see

101

what was wrong with it. As far as Sally can tell, there is not one word to indicate there is anything wrong with the paper. This is the third paper that Sally has got back with a C and nothing else on it. She wonders if Mrs. Literate has even read her papers. If there is nothing wrong with them, she should have an A. Sally feels very frustrated because she wants better grades but she does not know what to do to improve. She has done her best, and all she can get is a C.

Victor Victim has a new Irish setter puppy. Victor is going to build a kennel in the backyard as soon as he saves the money to buy the materials. Meanwhile, the dog is running all over the yard. It has been getting through a hole in the fence and going into Mrs. Neighbor's flower beds. Victor has tried to patch up the holes, but the puppy is small and can dig holes in the ground under the broken spot in the fence, and it is impossible to keep him from digging around any patches that are put in. Mrs. Neighbor is very angry and has been shooing the puppy away with a broom. Yesterday she hit the dog and Victor saw her and shouted, "Don't hit my dog!"

"Don't tell me what to do, young man. This dog is destroying my flowers. I am going to call animal control if he gets over here again!"

Coping with Teachers

Parents are the closest adults you must deal with, but many other adults influence your life. The next highest on your aggravation list is likely to be teachers. You are required to spend six or seven hours a day with teachers who may be extremely conscious of society's hierarchy. Some teachers believe that when they are at school and wearing their label of teacher, they are on an even higher rung of the hierarchical ladder. Because they are "teacher," they expect students to behave the way they are *supposed* to behave. In addition these people who believe they deserve unqualified respect sometimes do not show respect for their students.

Coping with sarcasm. Mr. Zero is a very sarcastic man, and he puts students down constantly. He does not treat them with dignity and respect, and students like Scott Scoffer openly defy him and treat him disrespectfully. Scott has not yet figured out, however, that when he treats Mr. Zero disrespectfully, Mr. Zero stays in the classroom and continues business as usual while Scott ends up in the office.

Mr. Zero will continue embarrassing and humiliating students until they let him know how they feel. Scott needed to get in touch with his feelings of hurt and embarrassment. His anger covered up his real feelings. Mr. Zero labeled Scott a tough and a smart mouth and has no idea that the angry response was Scott's reaction to feeling humiliated before his peers. Rather than the undignified name-calling, Scott needs to go to Mr. Zero after class and say, "Mr. Zero, it was really embarrassing to be called stupid in front of the class today." Teachers like Mr. Zero need to know that their behavior is disrespectful to students, and they need to learn that fact in a way that does not show disrespect for them. It must be done in such a way that teachers look at their own behavior rather than being angry about the behavior of the student.

Whenever you have been treated disrespectfully, swallow the nasty retort you want to scream back. You do not have to do anything right at that moment. You need to give yourself time to get in touch with what you are feeling. See the teacher after class or before class the next day and say, "I felt embarrassed and humiliated when I was called lazy in front of the class." As long as you have expressed your feelings in a calm, respectful way, you are okay. The teacher may say something sarcastic, apologize, or be totally speechless. If a sarcastic remark is made, simply say, "I just wanted to express my feelings. Thank you for listening." Do not go any further with it. You have taken care of yourself. If the teacher wants to pursue it, calls you smart aleck, or gets angry, you can say, "I'm sorry you're upset. I just wanted to express my feelings." You are taking care of yourself without attacking the teacher, and when you use "I" messages, you are owning your feelings and are in control of yourself. The "I" statement has positive power for expressing your feelings appropriately. It helps you and the person who mistreated you to focus on the real issue rather than getting involved in hurtful name-calling. It surprises and disarms the teacher and offers you an opportunity to express your feelings in a positive, acceptably assertive way.

Opening positive discussion. Sally Simmer has problems with teachers, too, but hers are generally a result of being nonassertive. She is often overlooked, but some of the more sensitive teachers have appreciated Sally's conscientiousness and have worked with her outside of class. With the extra attention, Sally's academic work improved dramatically in those classes. Sally does not participate in her English class, answering questions only those few times she is asked. Mrs. Literate does not know Sally personally. To her, Sally is a quiet girl in her third-period class.

She does not spend much time on Sally's papers and finds nothing special about them to comment on. Sally is frustrated by her seeming lack of progress in English. If she is to get any attention and make sure that Mrs. Literate does read her papers carefully, Sally must open the discussion with Mrs. Literate. She does not need the full Three-Step Plan, but she can use Step 1 and own the problem.

> SALLY: Mrs. Literate, I have a problem that I'd like your help with. I worked very hard on my last English composition, and I thought I had done an especially good job. I got a C, but there aren't any corrections or notes on the paper. I thought maybe you could show me what's wrong with it so I can do better next time.
> MRS. LITERATE: I don't remember your paper well enough to discuss it right now, Sally. Why don't you come in after school, and we'll look it over together.

An aggressively said, "Why did I get a C?" would have brought a response of "The paper deserved a C" and that would have been the end of the discussion. Anger would have been added to Sally's feeling of being treated unfairly. The assertive owning of the problem and asking for help puts Mrs. Literate in the position of being a helper, which is what she considers to be her primary function.

If Sally follows through and goes to see Mrs. Literate, you can be sure that her next paper will be read with care because Mrs. Literate will have invested part of herself in Sally's work.

Using the hierarchy. You may be thinking that not all teachers are helpful. You may stay after school to get special help, but you may have a teacher like Mr. Zero. Patsy Pushover went to him for help, but even then she could not understand his explanations of math. Do you have to "tough it out" if that happens? Of course not! However, at this point the student usually gives up on the teacher and tries to get help from a friend or complains a lot and does nothing to solve the problem. This is the time to put the hierarchy to work for you. You need the help of an adult, not a peer. The logical choice is your school counselor, but a teacher with whom you have a good relationship is a good choice, too. When Patsy finally realized that she was not going to do any better in math, she went to see Mr. Mentor about her problem.

PATSY: Mr. Mentor, I have a problem and I hope you can help me with it.

MR. MENTOR: So do I, Patsy. What is it?

PATSY: I'm having trouble in math. I don't understand Mr. Zero's explanations. I asked him for help and stayed after school twice, but it didn't do any good.

MR. MENTOR: What do you mean it didn't do any good?

PATSY: Well, I tried to pay close attention so I could follow Mr. Zero, but he'd lose me. When I asked him to go over it again, he'd get really mad and say I wasn't listening. I *was* listening. I was trying really hard to understand, but it was no use. He said I'll never learn math.

MR. MENTOR: Do you believe that, Patsy?

PATSY: I don't want to, but it sure seems like it might be true.

MR. MENTOR: Your record shows you got a C the first report period. How did you manage to keep up?

PATSY: Melody helped me a lot, but she doesn't have time to spend with me now. I don't know what I'm going to do.

MR. MENTOR: I don't want you to drop math, and Mr. Zero's class is the only one we can fit into your schedule. Let me ask around. We can probably find you a student math tutor. Mr. Calculator usually knows who can help. If he doesn't know of someone, I think Mrs. Diligent in the dean's office might know about tutors. We'll find you some help, Patsy.

PATSY: Thanks, Mr. Mentor.

The same conversation could have happened with a teacher, the librarian, the vice-principal, the coach, or any other adult at school who would be willing to help you. There is *always* someone on the school campus who knows how to get you the help you need. You do not have to "tough it out" or "go it alone." Teachers, counselors, administrators, and even the nonteaching staff want to help you. Take advantage of your opportunities to put the hierarchy to work for you.

Coping with Relatives

Fred Friendly is experiencing something that is quite common: judgmental grandparents. Fred is not going to cut his hair above his ears the way his grandfather wants him to, and it look as if Grandfather is not going to be quiet until he does. Fred is getting angry and resentful and is avoiding his grandfather to keep from saying something he will regret. This nonassertive behavior is not helping the situation because Fred's attitude toward his grandfather is becoming very negative. It does not look as if Fred can do anything about the situation without telling his grandfather to get off his case. Fred can do just that, and he has two ways to do it. The aggressive way would very likely go like this.

FRED: Grandpa, can't you stop talking about my hair?
GRANDFATHER: No, I can't, Fred. I just can't believe your parents would allow you to wear your hair like that. No son of mine would have his hair down over his ears.
FRED: Well, I'm not your son so you don't have to worry about it.
GRANDFATHER: That's no way to talk to your grandfather. I have a genuine concern about you because you're my grandson.
FRED: You don't have to be concerned about my hair. It's mine, and I can wear it any way I want.
GRANDFATHER: Now, see here, I don't like smart talk like that, young man.

The discussion can go on until Fred and his grandfather are both shouting and feeling so hostile that their relationship is ruined. Fred does have another alternative if he chooses to be assertive.

FRED: Grandpa, you know you've always been special to me, but lately I've been feeling real uncomfortable around you.
GRANDFATHER: I'm sorry to hear that, Fred. What's wrong?
FRED: I know you don't like my hair the way it is, but every time you see me you make a comment about it.
GRANDFATHER: I haven't made a secret of how I feel about a boy with long hair.
FRED: Grandpa, I understand how you feel. I'd like you to understand how I feel. When I'm put down all the time, I feel that I'm not liked any more, and I feel like hiding so I don't have to listen to the criticism. I'm not going to cut my hair, Grandpa, and I wish you could accept me the way I am.
GRANDFATHER: Why, Fred, I had no idea you felt so bad. I think you're trying to tell me to be quiet about your hair. I get the message. I'd like to be friends, too.

Suppose Grandfather were not so reasonable.

GRANDFATHER: If you don't want to be criticized, get that hair cut!
FRED: I'm not going to cut my hair, Grandpa.
GRANDFATHER: Well, I'm not going to be quiet about it until you do.
FRED: I'm sorry to hear that, Grandpa.

No matter what Grandfather's answer is, Fred will say no more because he has expressed his feelings. Since Grandfather knows Fred's feeling about being constantly criticized, Fred can choose how much time he spends around his grandparents. If his grandfather comments that Fred seems to avoid him, Fred can say, "I feel uncomfortable because my hair is criticized." He does not need to say anything else.

Grandparents are not the only relatives who can be a problem. Aunts, uncles, and older cousins sometimes seem to want to run your life. They feel the need to tell you what to do and to criticize. You can often fog away criticism or agree with it or both.

AUNT BIDDY: That blouse looks like you slept in it.
RITA: It's wrinkled all right.

AUNT BIDDY: You should help your mother more.
KEVIN: You're right.

AUNT BIDDY: You shouldn't treat your sister like that.
RUBY: You're probably right.

AUNT BIDDY: You're never on time!
FRED: It probably seems that way to you.

AUNT BIDDY: You're supposed to be out cutting the grass.
RANDY: You may be right.

You cannot change the Aunt Biddies of the world, but often by agreeing with them you can turn them off. They only know how to argue, so agreement ends their conversation. Sometimes relatives are very bossy and tell you what to do. Being ordered around by an uncle or a cousin can be infuriating. Your best bet is a calm, assertive "I" message. Use very low-level muscle, but be firm.

UNCLE BRUISER: C'mon, Leadbottom. Bring that wheel-barrow over so we can get on with the work.
VERNON: I don't mind helping, Uncle Bruiser, but I feel resentful being ordered around and called Leadbottom.
UNCLE BRUISER: Oh, you don't like being called Leadbottom.
VERNON: I feel put down.
UNCLE BRUISER: You're too thin-skinned getting huffy about something like that.
VERNON: You're probably right, but that's how I feel.

Uncle Bruiser may think that Vernon is too sensitive, but he will probably stop calling him Leadbottom. If he coninues by calling Vernon other names or being nasty about Vernon's sensitivity, Vernon needs to put the hierarchy to work.

VERNON: Dad, I have a problem that I think you can help me with.
DAD: What is it, Vernon?
VERNON: Uncle Bruiser has been calling me Leadbottom, and I told him I felt put down when he ordered me around and called me that. He said I was too thin-skinned and has been worse ever since. He's been real sarcastic and calls me Fragile Freda. I'm getting really mad, Dad, and I want to tell him off, but I know that would be bad idea.
DAD: I didn't realize he was being that hard on you, Vernon. I know how he can be. I'll talk to him and tell him to lay off.

Getting his dad to talk to Uncle Bruiser is a good idea for Vernon. Dad can say things to Bruiser as a peer that Vernon cannot say because of his youth. Fathers feel protective of their sons and feel it is part of their job description of father to help in such situations. Vernon did not ask Dad to do the job for him. He had already tried to cope with Uncle Bruiser assertively. He needed a little more muscle, and he needed muscle that Bruiser would accept. Dad was the right level of muscle for Vernon to use.

Just as with everyone else, when coping with relatives it is important that you feel good about yourself and the way you have handled the situation. Assertiveness is the way to cope with dignity and respect.

Coping with Employers

When you get your first job, it is very exciting. In the beginning it is all so new that you do not notice when things are not quite right. Kay Kind liked answering the phone and scheduling appointments in Aunt Harrie's salon. She liked to see the people come in with their hair looking one way and leave with it looking another. The first payday Kay was not paid on time she figured that Aunt Harrie had forgotten her because she was new on the payroll, but she has been there over seven weeks now. Aunt Harrie knows she is there and for some reason is not paying her on time. What can Kay do? It is humiliating to ask for money even when you have earned it. Kay needs to use the Three-Step Plan with Aunt Harrie to plan how she will be paid on time.

KAY: Aunt Harrie, I have a problem and I need your help.
AUNT HARRIE: Oh, how can I help, Kay?
KAY: This is really hard for me to talk about. I feel uncomfortable bringing up the subject, but I need to have a clear understanding of how I'm to be paid.
AUNT HARRIE: Am I behind again, Kay? It just slipped my mind.
KAY: Yes, Aunt Harrie. I was supposed to be paid last week.
AUNT HARRIE: Last week! Oh, I'm sorry. I'll pay you right now.
KAY: That's only part of it. I'd like to set up a way to handle my payday that would be easy for you and for me, too.
AUNT HARRIE: Well, I don't have an idea on that right now.
KAY: I have a plan that might work. How about if on payday I put my time card right in the middle of your desk with the hours totaled and the amount due. Then you would know that it is payday for me and you wouldn't even have to figure it up. You could check my figures and it would just take you a minute.
AUNT HARRIE: That sounds good to me. (Laughing.) I suppose you have your time card all ready for me.
KAY: (With a smile.) As a matter of fact, I do.

Since Kay and Aunt Harrie were friends, it may seem that it would have been easier than if she did not know her employer personally. Asking for your money is hard, no matter how well you know your employer. If you use the Three-Step Plan and have good alternatives ready, your employer will listen to you. Employers sometimes think it is not important to pay young people on time. You need to let your employer know that payday is important to you. Evaluate your situation and come up with a plan that will make it easy for you to remind your employer that it is payday and hard for him to forget. Kay's idea of putting the time card where Aunt Harrie could not miss seeing it is good. You could mark the calendar, especially if your employer turns the page daily. Be creative and come up with an idea that he cannot refuse.

Young people who work in fast-food restaurants will have managers of varying degrees of ability. Some managers are very poor organizers, and scheduling hours for employees can be haphazard and very irregular. You may be left off of the work roster or get only five or six hours a week. Talking to Mr. Manager is a problem. Before you talk to him, know what you want and have a plan to offer him.

Stan Stabel worked at a hamburger franchise. When he was hired, his employer promised him twelve to fifteen hours per week. Last week Stan was scheduled for six hours and was called late Friday afternoon to work all day Saturday. Because he did not expect to work Saturday, Stan had made plans to spend the day with friends. This was not the first time Stan had had to change plans because he was called to work at the last minute, and he was feeling very angry about it. Stan wanted to keep his job, but he also wanted to know what hours and what days he would be working. He decided to talk to Mr. Manager.

STAN: Mr. Manager, I have a problem, and I think you can help me with it.
MR. MANAGER: What is it, Stan?
STAN: When I was hired, our agreement was that I would work twelve to fifteen hours a week.
MR. MANAGER: That's right.
STAN: I haven't had regular hours at all. Last week I was only scheduled for six hours, and then I was called at the last minute to work on Saturday.
MR. MANAGER: Somebody got sick, and we needed you.
STAN: I don't mind being called in once in a while, but I would like to be scheduled to work regular hours during the week.
MR. MANAGER: You know it's hard to promise you particular days during the week.

STAN: I don't need particular days. I would just like twelve to fifteen hours regularly. It would help me plan my budget.
MR. MANAGER: I see what you mean, Stan. I didn't realize your hours had been that irregular. I'll keep you in mind when I make up the roster this week.

Mr. Manager may or may not make an effort to give Stan twelve hours. Stan did assertively set forth his needs. He did not tell Mr. Manager that his method for setting hours was stupid and the person doing the roster was incapable; he simply stuck to what he needed. If Mr. Manager does not give him twelve hours regularly, Stan can begin looking for another job, and he will be able to use Mr. Manager as a reference and to give as his reason for leaving the job that he wanted to work more hours. Stan's assertiveness may pay off with regular hours from Mr. Manager, but if it does not, he will have taken care of his needs with dignity and respect.

Coping with Other Adults

Victor and his puppy are not doing well with Mrs. Neighbor right now. Victor is one of those people who always seem to be in some kind of bad spot. If he leaves the rake out, you can be sure Mom will run over it with the car. When he got the dog, Victor promised to build the dog run right away, but the materials were more expensive than he expected, so he has had to save for a few weeks more. The puppy is a lot livelier than Victor had at first thought. It has been a job keeping the puppy out of Mrs. Neighbor's yard, and Victor is not always around to watch the dog. Since he does not want Mrs. Neighbor to hit his dog, he needs to own the problem and to open discussion with Mrs. Neighbor.

VICTOR: Mrs. Neighbor, I have a problem and I'd like your help. I've saved my money for a year to buy an Irish setter. My pup is really active and sometimes he gets out of the yard. I'm going to build him a good kennel as soon as I can save the money to buy the materials. Until then he may get out of the yard sometimes. It would really help me if you would call me if he gets out and gets into your yard. Then I can come and get him right away. I don't want him to bother you or get into your flowerbeds.

MRS. NEIGHBOR: Well, he *is* getting into my flowerbeds.
VICTOR: Please call me when he does that and I'll get him.
I'm trying to keep the hole in the fence patched, but he keeps
digging around it.
MRS. NEIGHBOR: I know he does. I put some wood there,
too, and he still gets through. I wish you would hurry up and get
that kennel done.
VICTOR: It won't be long. Don't forget to call me when the
puppy bothers you. Thanks.

Mrs. Neighbor is still going to be angry, but she and Victor did
not fight. She can call Victor and complain to him. Victor knows
that is what she will do, so he does not mind since he expects it. It
is his problem until the kennel is built.

There are adults all around you who can be a problem.
Sometimes people on the street say rude things to you. You are
never going to see those people again. Why even bother with
them? It is not worth your energy. Save your energy for times
when it is important. The woman in the school attendance office
who is always so sharp with you when you come in from a dental
appointment may need an "I" statement. "I feel that I'm doing
something that irritates you. Is something wrong?" Her feet may
hurt, and she may not realize that she is speaking so sharply. She
will probably tell you that everything is fine and that you are not
doing anything wrong. Next time you come in she will probably
have something pleasant to say.

If a salesperson in a store is rude to you, check yourself first.
Were you behaving impolitely? What did you do, and how did you
do it? What did you say, and how did you say it? Check your body
language. Your tone of voice or voice volume could be irritating
the salesperson. If he is taking other people ahead of you, all you
have to say is, "I'm next," or "It's my turn now." If a salesperson
is ignoring you, say, "I'd like some help, please." If a salesperson
says, "You kids are all alike. You handle everything and throw it
down any which way," your response could be, "Some kids may
be careless and messy, but I haven't been throwing things
around."

If adults are rude to you, there is no need for you to be rude in
return. If they infringe on your rights, use an "I" statement to let
them know how you are feeling or what you need. Agree with the
truth and disagree with what is not true. Fog away criticism when
appropriate. Open positive discussion by owning the problem. Use

the hierarchy to help you when you need to. You have many choices for coping with adults appropriately.

Giving Positive Attention

It is always easy to see what is wrong with someone else, especially adults. Mr. Zero is sarcastic. Mrs. Neighbor is a grouch. Grandfather is critical. The list could go on and on because as long as you are looking for negative things, you will find them.

When you focus on negative behavior, your own behavior becomes more negative. Every time you complain about adults, you have sent out a negative message. You have added negative energy to the situation. Nothing positive will be accomplished because positive results cannot come out of negative energy. It is time to stop that flow of negative energy and replace it with a flow of positive energy.

Even though he seems unreasonable and sarcastic, there are some good things to be said about Mr. Zero: he gets tests back to students the day after they're given. Mrs. Neighbor has the prettiest flowers on the street because she works so hard taking care of them. When Mr. Zero returns the math tests, he needs to hear, "It sure is nice to have the test back the day after we take it. Thanks, Mr. Zero." When Mrs. Neighbor is working in her yard, Victor could say, "Your hard work really pays off, Mrs. Neighbor; your yard always looks nice." Fred told his grandfather, "You know you've always been special to me." Grandfather needed to hear that. The next time an Aunt Biddy bakes her chocolate cake, she needs to hear, "You make terrific chocolate cake, Aunt Biddy."

By expressing positive things, you get positive energy flowing. Do not expect positive back from the adults. Give your positive strokes for free because you want to feel good by being positive. You are giving the strokes for yourself and to yourself even more than for or to the other person. The other person can reject the positive comment. That is okay. You are doing this for yourself. You want to be positive. Work on thinking positively and expressing positive thoughts to adults for a month, and then sit down and ask yourself what is happening. The answer will be pleasantly surprising to you.

CHAPTER X

Coping with Other Young People

Oscar Ordinary's brother Hector is only nine, but he is a big pain as far as Oscar is concerned. Hector tries to blackmail Oscar by saying, "I'm gonna tell." Oscar usually snarls back, "Go ahead, you little creep. You're always spying and trying to get me in trouble!" He generally grabs Hector and pushes him down on the bed or the sofa, not to hurt him but to show who is boss. Hector gets into Oscar's things and will not stay out of his room. Oscar has asked his parents if he can put a lock on his door to keep Hector out, but his parents say he is making a big deal out of nothing. Hector's latest foray into Oscar's room ended with Oscar's favorite model airplane being broken. Oscar would have done something serious if Hector had not gone running to their father. Mr. Ordinary had been angry with Oscar for mistreating Hector but did not say one word to Hector about breaking the model.

Patrick Pushover is having a hard time coping with Kevin Kombat. Kevin not only cuts in front of Patrick at lunch, but also has begun making cruel remarks to him and calling him Patricia. Kevin thinks he is being funny, but Patrick is not laughing. When Patrick walked by Kevin's desk in Spanish, Kevin stuck his foot out to trip him. When Patrick stumbled, Kevin told him he had better get his glasses changed so he could see where he was going. After a series of incidents like that over the past few months, Patrick is hurt and angry, but he does not know how to handle the situation.

Barry Belligerent considers himself a "Rocker." He hates "Mods," "Breakers," and "New Wavers." He can take "Punkers" all right if they do not try to push him. Barry has nothing good to say about "Jocks" and "Preppies," and the farther "Dexters" stay from him, the better. Greg Garious and Joe Veal, whom Barry considers to be "Mods," are in four of Barry's classes. They stay away from him, and he thinks he knows why. They are snobs and think they are superior to him because of the way he dresses and the kind of music he likes. Barry thinks the music Greg and Joe listen to is sick. He knows what they think of him because they got up and left the table when he sat down in the cafeteria one day. In the hall Joe accidentally bumped into Barry. Barry snarled, "Watch who you're bumpin' into, Mod. You'll get this if you don't watch out," and slammed his right fist against his left palm with a loud crack.

Ima Imposer and Tracy Carbon have been going together for two months. Ima confuses Tracy. One minute she is all smiles and hanging on him like ivy on a wall, and the next minute she will not talk to him. When he asks her what is wrong, she says, "Nothing." Tracy knows by the tone of her voice, the expression on her face, and the way she lifts up her chin and looks the other way that something is definitely wrong.

Coping with Younger Brothers and Sisters

Little brothers and sisters can be a serious problem when they do not know their place in the hierarchy. Little brothers are *supposed* to do what big brothers tell them to do. Unfortunately, the hierarchy seems to get turned around for big brothers. Parents think that big brothers are *supposed* to take care of little brothers, be tolerant of them because they are younger, and never mistreat them in any way. The hierarchy does not give the advantage to older brothers but to the younger ones in many families. That is certainly the way it seems to work in the Ordinary family. Oscar has not only his little brother to deal with, but also his parents' attitude.

Before Oscar can do anything about the problem, he has to look at himself. How is he contributing to the problem? Oscar is yelling at his brother, pushing him around, calling him names, threatening him, and complaining to their parents about him. When Oscar knows how he is contributing to the problem, he can stop doing those things. He needs to replace that behavior with more positive behavior. You are thinking that Hector will still be a pain. Forget Hector's behavior. Oscar cannot change Hector. He can only change Oscar. He needs to cope with Hector with assertiveness. He needs to start expressing his feelings and needs in "I" statements. "Hector, I'm really mad because my airplane is broken. I feel real bad because that was my favorite model. I'm so mad I want you to go away right now because I want to hit you for breaking my plane."

Oscar needs to plan for coping with Hector. He also needs his parents' help if he is to be successful in changing his relationship with Hector. He needs to tell his parents how he plans to deal with

Hector and ask them to support him. Here is Oscar's Three-Step Plan for coping with Hector assertively.

Step 1.   Own the problem and ask for help.
   OSCAR: Mom and Dad, I have a problem and I want you to help me with it.
   DAD: What do you need, Oscar?
   OSCAR: I'm having a hard time with Hector. The latest thing he did was break my favorite model. I know that I've done some pretty mean things to him. I'm trying to stop yelling at him and calling him names, and I don't want to push him around anymore. I really do want to make things better.
   MOM: I'm glad to hear that, Oscar. It sounds like you're trying to be more responsible toward your brother.
   DAD: You said you wanted us to help you. How can we help?

Step 2.   Offer alternatives.
   OSCAR: Well, Dad, I'm going to talk to Hector and tell him that I'd like us to be friends. I want to come up with a plan that he and I can agree on. I think we can work things out together. When we get our agreement worked out, I want to show it to you both to be sure you know what we've agreed on. Once we all understand the agreement between Hector and me, I need you to agree not to get involved in what goes on between us.
   MOM: Now, just a minute, Oscar. We can't let you treat Hector any way you want to and not get involved.
   OSCAR: Mom, I'm not going to hurt Hector. I'm going to be real nice to him, and you'll know what our agreement is. You know he has a bad habit of saying things to get me in trouble...
   MOM: Oscar!
   OSCAR: Well, it's true. Then if you take his side he comes and smirks at me and thinks he's big. If we're going to get along, Hector has to learn to deal with me, and I have to deal with him. If he runs to you all the time, we won't be able to work things out.
   MOM: That sounds like expecting a lot from a nine-year-old.
   DAD: I think I see what you're driving at, Oscar. You don't want Hector to do something and then come running to us and hide behind us.
   OSCAR: That's it, Dad.
   MOM: Well, I'm still not sure.

Step 3.   Be willing to negotiate.
   OSCAR: Could we try it for two weeks, Mom? That would give
me a chance to see if it works.
   DAD: I agree to that.
   OSCAR: So when Hector comes running to you telling you
something about me, you'll tell him he has to talk to me about it
and you're sure we can work it out.
   DAD: Okay, we can do that.
   OSCAR: Thanks. I'll go talk to Hector now.

                              *   *   *
   OSCAR: Hector, come 'ere. I want to talk to you.
   HECTOR: Are you still mad about the plane?
   OSCAR: I'm still mad, but I don't want to hit you anymore. In
fact, I want to stop fighting with you.
   HECTOR: You do?
   OSCAR: Yeah. I'd like to work out an agreement with you on
how we can keep from fighting.
   HECTOR: Okay, I won't fight anymore.
   OSCAR: Well, there's more to it than that. I have a list of all
the things you do that I don't want you to do so you'll know
exactly what I don't like. You can make a list of all the things
you don't want me to do. Then we'll see if we can work out a
way to get along together.
   HECTOR: I don't want you to hit me and call me a creep.
   OSCAR: Wait a minute. Here's my list. Look at it first and
then we'll do your list.
   HECTOR: (Seeing "stay out of my room".) I like to go in your
room because you got neat stuff. That's why I go in there. I
know it makes you mad, but I like to go in.
   OSCAR: Okay, how about if I say stay out of my room unless
I'm home and say you can go in?
   HECTOR: You never let me in when you're home.
   OSCAR: Well, if you promise to stay out other times, I'll let
you in sometimes.
   HECTOR: You promise?
   OSCAR: I promise. If you stay out until Saturday, I'll let you
come in an' help me when I straighten everything up. (Oscar
figures he can get a little help cleaning his room.)
   HECTOR: Okay. And if I don't go in your room and don't tell
on you and agree to the stuff on the list, you won't push me
around and yell at me.
   OSCAR: Right. You have to stop calling me names too.

Oscar and Hector go through Oscar's list and then make a list of Hector's wants for Oscar. They agree how they will treat each other. When the lists are completed and changes negotiated, they take the agreement to their parents, and Oscar gives them a copy to keep, too. An important part of the agreement is that if one of them slips up, he will apologize to the other. If they are angry with each other, they will express their anger verbally in an appropriate way—no more name-calling. Oscar can teach Hector how to use "I" messages by modeling them. When Hector hears, "I am really mad because my baseball glove was left outside," and "I was embarrassed when Suzy was here and you told her I had her picture pinned on my wall," Hector will begin to say, "I get really mad when I'm watching TV and you tell me to go away just because your friends come over."

Things will not go perfectly, but Oscar can make his world more peaceful by being assertive. His owning the problem and asking his parents for help, suggesting an alternative to the present fighting, and being willing to negotiate with his parents and with his brother have opened a new way of handling problems in his family.

You can take the responsibility for improving your relationship with your brothers and sisters *if you want to*. You can begin by pretending they are strangers and you have to treat them politely. The foundation of your relationship must be dignity and respect, and you maintain that by expressing your feelings, wants, and needs in "I" statements. Many problems with sisters and brothers are recurring problems. You need to make up one "I" statement to use every time your brother calls you Bug Eyes: "I feel put down when I'm called Bug Eyes." For a sister who takes things, try "I don't want you to take my things without asking me." "I feel resentful when I'm left to clean the kitchen by myself," lets your brother know that he has let you down.

"I" messages take care of you at a low level of muscle. If you need more muscle, you can work on a Three-Step Plan with your parents and your sister or brother. Use the hierarchy to help you, but be sure that you are willing to clean up your act and treat others and yourself with dignity and respect.

Coping with Peers

Patrick Pushover is very easy to intimidate. It makes him an easy mark for people who like to have fun at the expense of others or for those who take advantage of nonassertive people. Kevin does not want to hurt Patrick physically, but he does take advantage of him and torments him. It does not occur to Kevin that Patrick might feel hurt or humiliated.

It will be very difficult for Patrick to stand up to Kevin, but Kevin must be told that he is being cruel. As long as Kevin is not confronted, he will continue to harass Patrick. Inside, the Real Kevin knows that he is tormenting Patrick, but his Voice tells him that Patrick's reactions are funny and no harm is done. Patrick cannot make wise comments back to Kevin because Kevin can roll right over him with aggressiveness.

Patrick has been talking with Mr. Mentor about his problems with Kevin, and Mr. Mentor has been working with him to help him become more assertive. Patrick has decided that the next time Kevin wants to cut in line, he will say, "I'm not giving cuts today." Also, if Kevin calls him Patricia, he will say, "My name is Patrick." Patrick has practiced with a tape recorder to hear how he sounds, and he has said his "I" message in front of the mirror to see how he looks. He is going to be like a broken record and will not argue with Kevin. Patrick is ready to be assertive.

KEVIN: Hi, Patricia. Thanks for saving my place.
PATRICK: (Standing straight and speaking firmly.) My name is Patrick, and I'm not giving cuts today.
KEVIN: (Surprised.) Well, I'm just getting a milkshake, *Patrick*.
PATRICK: I'm not giving cuts today.
KEVIN: C'mon, you always give me cuts.
PATRICK: I'm not giving cuts today.
KEVIN: Well, what're you gonna do about it?
PATRICK: I'm not giving cuts today.
KEVIN: You sound serious.
PATRICK: I am serious.
KEVIN: You know, if I want to I can stand here whether you like it or not.
PATRICK: I'm not giving cuts today.
KEVIN: All right! Cheez, you don't have to make such a big deal about it. (Walks away.)

If Kevin comes to cut in line again, Patrick knows he can handle it, and from now on any time Kevin calls him Patricia, he will say, "My name is Patrick." When Kevin has stopped cutting in line and calling him Patricia, Patrick will work on the other put-downs and wise remarks that Kevin likes to make. He has decided to say, "I think that was a put-down. It hurt my feelings and I don't like it." That is much more difficult, and Patrick has practiced it over and over. He is finally ready.

When passing Patrick in the hall, Kevin bumped into him on purpose and said, "Oops! Those glasses are getting worse."

PATRICK: I think that was a put-down. It hurt my feelings and I don't like it.
KEVIN: You sure can't take a joke.
PATRICK: I think that was a put-down. It hurt my feelings and I don't like it.
KEVIN: Hey, man, I didn't mean nothin'.

In Spanish class Kevin did his little tripping move again.

KEVIN: (Snickering.) Oh, pardon me.
PATRICK: I think that was a put-down. It hurt my feelings, and I don't like it.
KEVIN: Poor Patrick, your feelings are hurt. Don't be so sensitive.

Patrick did not pick up the bait but went to his seat. A few days later, Kevin gave it one last whirl.

KEVIN: Your feet having trouble walking, Patrick?
PATRICK: I think that was a put-down. It hurt my feelings, and I don't like it.
KEVIN: You sure can't take a joke anymore.
PATRICK: I don't think it was a joke. I think it was a put-down...
KEVIN: I know, I know. You don't like it. Okay, okay. (Shaking his head.)

Patrick could not hope to overpower Kevin so he did not try, but he certainly could outlast him. Kevin gave up because of Patrick's persistence. Patrick's heart pounded every time, but he was dignified in his handling of himself and Kevin. Kevin was treated respectfully, and assertiveness gave Patrick what he needed to stop his tormentor.

Barry Belligerent has separated and labeled everyone. Those people who fit into categories he finds unacceptable, he considers enemies. They do not have to do anything. They merely have to be placed in a category by Barry to have all of the negative characteristics he has given to the category. Since he rejects so many people, Barry feels that others reject him, that others are "out to get him," so he is very defensive: He is going to get others before they get him.

Greg and Joe think Barry is okay, but he gets loud and aggressive sometimes. One day he came into the cafeteria cussing New Wavers. When he sat down at their table, Joe and Greg were so embarrassed they left. Barry insists on calling them Mods even though they do not consider themselves members of any group. Things have seemed to be getting worse lately, and Barry threatened to hit Joe when he accidentally bumped into Barry in the hall. Since Barry is in so many of their classes, he seems to be singling them out for comments about Mods and what he would like to do to Mods. They are feeling very uncomfortable about him and are not sure they can handle him by themselves, but they would like to to talk with him and settle the differences he seems to have with them.

In truth, Barry's problems with other people are all inside him. He has an aggressive Voice that rules him. The Real Barry does not have a chance. Barry has no idea how aggressive his behavior appears to other people. He is angry at everything in general and can become angry at anyone in particular he thinks is offending him. Barry's aggressive behavior has caused several teachers to refer him to Mr. Mentor. After talking with him several times, Mr. Mentor is not sure that Barry realizes that he is manufacturing his own problems with others.

Joe and Greg do not want to continue the growing tension between them and Barry, so they go to see Mr. Mentor.

JOE: Mr. Mentor, we're having a problem with Barry Belligerent.

MR. MENTOR: Tell me about it.

GREG: We think Barry is an all-right guy. He gets loud and says things that embarrass us, but we thought he was okay until he started calling us Mods and making cracks about us.

JOE: He hates everybody who isn't a Rocker, and all he talks about anymore is "getting" New Wavers or Mods or Jocks. We're in four classes with him, and it's getting pretty bad. He threatened to hit me the other day when I accidentally bumped into him.

GREG: We'd like to get things straightened out with him. We're not sure why he doesn't like us, but we sure don't want him getting any madder at us.

MR. MENTOR: Are you willing to tell him how you feel?

JOE: You mean go up to him and tell him?

MR. MENTOR: No, no. I mean if we had a meeting here in my office would you tell him?

GREG: I would as long as you were here with us.

JOE: Me, too.

MR. MENTOR: I've been working with Barry, but I don't think he understands how he affects people. You could help him if you tell him how you feel.

Mr. Mentor checks Barry's schedule to find what class he is in and sends for him. As soon as he sees Greg and Joe, Barry is on the defensive.

BARRY: I guess these two have been telling you what a bad guy I am. They're a couple of snobs and think they're better than me.

MR. MENTOR: Wait a minute, Barry. You may be way off base. They haven't been telling me what a bad guy you are, and they certainly don't think they're better than you.

BARRY: Oh, yeah, then why did they get up and walk away when I sat down at their table in the cafeteria?

JOE: I was embarrassed. You were yelling and cussing New Wavers, and it was embarrassing.

GREG: I didn't know what you would say when you sat down. I was afraid you might start cussing us and calling us Mods.

BARRY: Well, you didn't want to be around me.

GREG: Not when you're like that.

BARRY: You Mods don't want to be around a Rocker anyway.

JOE: I'm not a Mod.

BARRY: You look like one to me. You listen to Mod music.

JOE: I'm not a Mod, and I don't like being called one.

BARRY: You're just too good to be seen with a Rocker.

GREG: I never said that, Barry.

BARRY: You wouldn't sit with me in the cafeteria anyway because of the way I dress.

GREG: I don't judge people by how they dress. I'll sit with anybody.

BARRY: Well, you wouldn't sit with me.

GREG: It isn't the way you dress. I don't care if you have a ring in your nose if that's what you want. I feel embarrassed by the things you say and how you make such a big deal about other groups.

JOE: I don't like being called names. You called me a snob and a Mod and made fun of *my* clothes. I don't think I've done anything to deserve that.

BARRY: Just being a Mod deserves that.

MR. MENTOR: Barry, what did Joe say about the Mod thing?

BARRY: He said he's not a Mod.

MR. MENTOR: What have Joe and Greg done to you to deserve your attitude toward them?

BARRY: They just think they're better than me.

GREG: That's not true.

MR. MENTOR: How *do* you feel about Barry?

JOE: I think he's an all-right guy.

GREG: He was always okay with me before.

MR. MENTOR: How do you feel about his attitude toward you?

JOE: I really don't know what he's mad about.

MR. MENTOR: You're confused.

GREG: Yeah. We never did anything to make him so mad.

MR. MENTOR: Barry?

BARRY: I guess they didn't *do* anything.

MR. MENTOR: How do you feel about them now?

BARRY: I don't know.

MR. MENTOR: Can you stop the comments about Mods and the other stuff you've been saying to them?

BARRY: Yeah, I guess I can do that.

MR. MENTOR: How does that feel to you boys?

JOE: I'm okay with that.

GREG: Me, too. I'd really like things to be better.

MR. MENTOR: Okay, boys. Thanks for coming in, Barry. I'll give you passes back to class.

Mr. Mentor knows that Barry is still going to be angry, and he is not going to relax around Joe and Greg for a while. Mr. Mentor will call Barry in again in a few days and see if his attitude is any different. It will be difficult for Barry to accept what Joe and Greg have said about his behavior, but they did not attack him or put him down. They treated him with dignity and respect. They discussed the behavior that bothered them, and they expressed their feelings in an appropriate way.

The situation between Barry and Greg and Joe was "touchy" because of Barry's anger. Using the hierarchy to help was very important. This was a time when older, wiser counsel was needed. You do not need to "tough things out." The Mr. Mentors have helped others through similar difficult situations. Trust them to help you, too. Be assertive and ask for help when you need it.

Coping with the Opposite Sex

In looking at the situation with Tracy and Ima, it is hard to tell which one is having more difficulty. At first glance, it looks as though Ima is giving Tracy a bad time. He does not know what to do about the "silent treatment." Ima has learned to play "Guess what I'm feeling" very well. Her game could also be called "Guess why I'm mad." Tracy is guessing wrong, so things are not good. Tracy is so busy trying to guess what is going on with Ima that he is not in touch with his own feelings. Ima is putting so much energy into being angry because Tracy is not guessing why she is angry that she does not realize that she is not expressing her feelings in a way that makes sense to Tracy.

Directly and honestly expressing yourself is the basis for clear communication. Quite often when you become involved in a romantic relationship you fall automatically into a framework of how you think couples "should" act when they go together. Ima's "should" puts claims on Tracy's behavior that he does not always live up to. In fact, Tracy does not know what Ima's "shoulds" are because she has never stated them. Ima is angry today because Tracy went to the movies with Randy and Kevin when he "should" have spent the time with her. She has been angry in the past because Tracy "should" call her every day, "should" not talk to other girls, "should" meet her for lunch every day, and "should" go out with her on Friday and Saturday nights.

Tracy did not know he was supposed to do all of those things. He does not always want to have lunch with Ima, and they had a big fight over that. Now, this hassle makes Tracy wonder if it is worth all the bother having a girlfriend. Girlfriends "should" not be so hard to get along with.

Ima and Tracy need to stop "shoulding" on each other and to begin expressing their wants and needs assertively—honestly and directly. Instead of being cold and distant when Tracy did not see her at lunch time, Ima could have handled it assertively.

IMA: I missed you at lunch today.
TRACY: Oh, I had lunch with the guys today.
IMA: I look forward to seeing you at lunch because you have practice after school.
TRACY: Sometimes I want to be with the guys at lunch.
IMA: I feel real rejected that you'd rather be with the guys than with me.
TRACY: I'm not rejecting you, Ima. I care about you a lot, but I don't see my friends as much as I used to, so once in a while I like to have lunch with them.
IMA: Are you mad at me or something?
TRACY: No. I just wanted to see the guys.
IMA: Next time would you tell me when you're not meeting me for lunch?
TRACY: Sure.

Ima may not be too pleased that Tracy wants to see his friends sometimes, but she can accept it. Tracy had an opportunity to state his wants and now knows how to treat Ima when he plans to do something with the guys. Ima needs to learn that although she thinks going with a boy means they "should" spend every spare minute together, that is not how real life works.

If Ima cannot be honest and direct with her feelings, Tracy can be. When Ima is giving him the "silent treatment," he needs to let her know how he feels.

TRACY: I'm really confused. I don't know what I did to make you mad and not talk to me.
IMA: Don't worry about it.
TRACY: Okay. I can't guess what's wrong, so I'll take your word for it and not worry about it.
IMA: You should know what's wrong.
TRACY: I can't know unless you tell me.
IMA: Just don't bother.
TRACY: I'm ready to listen if you want to tell me. If you don't, that's okay too. Let me know when I can help.

Tracy has treated Ima with dignity and respect. He has given her an open invitation to talk when she is ready. He is not playing the "Great American Guessing Game" any longer. Ima may sputter and complain, but she will have to tell Tracy what is wrong because he is through guessing.

A twist to the "Guess what I'm mad about" game is the "Guess what somebody else told me you did that I'm mad about" game. When Tracy was at a football game out of town, he was seen talking to the cheerleaders along with Kevin and Vernon. Ima's informant told her that Tracy looked really interested in the cute blonde cheerleader. At the bus after the game, Tracy and Kevin were writing down what looked like addresses and phone numbers. Ima was hurt, furious, and terribly jealous. When Tracy came by the next day, she would not talk to him for an hour. Finally, because he was getting ready to leave, she snarled at him.

IMA: I suppose you're going home to call that blonde?
TRACY: What blonde?
IMA: I heard about how you were so interested in that cheerleader yesterday.
TRACY: What?
IMA: I know you were talking to the cheerleaders yesterday.
TRACY: Yeah, I was talking to the cheerleaders.
IMA: And you thought the blonde was really cute.
TRACY: They were all real fine.
IMA: And I suppose you're going to tell me you didn't get the blonde's phone number.
TRACY: No, I didn't get the blonde's phone number. I got her boyfriend's phone number because he's an old friend of mine.
IMA: Oh!
TRACY: You've been mad because someone told you I was talking to another girl yesterday and got her phone number. You didn't even ask me. You decided I was guilty because someone else told you. You really make me mad when you do that!
IMA: I'm sorry. I thought...
TRACY: You thought. Yeah, you thought the worst possible thing about me you could. You always think the worst.
IMA: You didn't tell me you knew her boyfriend.
TRACY: You didn't ask me. You just accused me of trying to start something with another girl.
IMA: Well, what would you think if someone told you I was giving my phone number to someone else?
TRACY: I hope I'd check it out with you before I made a big deal out of it.

Notice how the confrontation is full of "you" messages. Ima and Tracy are both accusing with "you" messages, and they are defensive as a result of having the "you" thrown at them. When a "you" message is delivered, the implication is that *you* are wrong. Couples get snarled up in attack and defense in an effort to be right. They never get to the issue of what they are feeling. Ima was feeling hurt and jealous. Tracy was feeling unjustly attacked and hurt. Instead of dealing with their feelings, Ima and Tracy were accusing each other of being wrong: Tracy for talking to the cheerleader, Ima for unjustly accusing Tracy and not checking with him to find out what actually happened. They never took care of their feelings, and Tracy ended up resentful and Ima contrite. Neither felt good. Neither treated the other with dignity and respect.

When Ima's "friend" gave her this delicious little piece of gossip, Ima needed to give Tracy the benefit of the doubt and check it out with him, being very assertively direct and honest.

IMA: Tracy, I heard something I need to check out with you. I was told you were talking to the cheerleaders yesterday, and it looked like you got a phone number from one of them.

TRACY: Oh, yeah, I was talking to the cheerleaders. One of them is going with an old friend of mine. He moved away when we were in fifth grade. She said that he had seen our roster and asked her to find out if I was the Tracy Carbon he knew in grade school. He had to work yesterday so he couldn't come to the game. I was real glad to get his phone number. I called him last night, and we're talking about getting together soon.

IMA: That's great!

What a difference in the conversation when Ima checked it out rather than making an assumption. She began with a very direct "I" statement. Tracy did not feel threatened and gave her a full explanation without further prompting.

Sometimes Tracy is not so easy to get along with either. He has a Firebird that he has been working on for months. The paint job is perfect, and he tells everyone to be careful when opening the doors so the paint will not get dinged. One night he was parked on a slope, and when Ima opened the door it slipped out of her hand and banged against a pole. Tracy came unglued and yelled at her in front of the other couple in the car. Ima was embarrassed and humiliated, and when Tracy would not stop, she yelled, "Just be quiet about it. I said I'm sorry. Get off my case!" Tracy finally shut up, but Ima was still embarrassed because he had yelled at her in front of the others, and she also felt bad about yelling back at him. Later Tracy felt especially bad because he had made such a big deal and nothing had happened to the car. If it had been handled assertively and Ima and Tracy had treated each other with dignity and respect, there would have been no uncomfortable feelings to live with afterward.

An assertive way for Ima to deal with Tracy's outburst would be to acknowledge and share her feelings. "It was an accident. I feel embarrassed being yelled at like this." If Tracy continued Ima would need to raise the muscle level and say, "I feel very embarrassed, Tracy, and I want you stop yelling at me. We can talk about it later." Such direct confrontation will most likely stop Tracy's outburst, and they can talk about the situation later.

Ending a relationship. In any couple relationship, you need to evaluate what is happening and decide how comfortable the relationship is. If it seems that you are always trying hard to make things work and they never get better, it may be that the relationship simply does not work and needs to be ended. Ending a relationship is always difficult, and few people know how to do it gracefully. You may stay together because you do not know how to end it without hurting the other person. It is unfair to both of you when you stay in a relationship because the other person might be hurt. It is dishonest, and it robs the other person of the opportunity to be involved with someone who can genuinely care for her/him.

Some people provoke a fight so they can break up. Others stop calling and seeing the other person and refuse to discuss the relationship because they cannot face the other person's pain from the breakup. You can assertively end a relationship by expressing your feelings honestly and directly.

TRACY: Ima, I need to talk to you.
IMA: Okay.
TRACY: I've been feeling really uncomfortable about us lately. I don't think we're making it as a couple.
IMA: Well, I'm trying real hard to be the way you want me to be.
TRACY: That's just it, Ima. I don't want you to have to try hard to be what I want. You're fine the way you are.
IMA: Then why do you want to break up?

TRACY: I can't handle being given the "silent treatment" all the time. I can't guess why you're mad at me because it's usually over something that I don't think is worth getting mad over. I need to be able to see my friends without feeling guilty because you expect me to be with you all the time. I feel all tied up.
IMA: I won't do that anymore. I'll change.
TRACY: I don't want you to change. I would rather not be together anymore.
IMA: But I like you so much.
TRACY: I like you, too, but I don't want to be together anymore.
IMA: Can't I do anything to change your mind?
TRACY: No.
IMA: I feel awful! (Crying.)
TRACY: I'm sorry about that. I really don't want to hurt you.
IMA: That doesn't help much.
TRACY: I feel bad that you feel bad, but I really feel this is best.

Tracy has been honest with Ima. He has told her what he cannot cope with in the relationship. He has treated her with dignity and respect. She is hurt, but Tracy has saved her from bigger hurt later. By continuing the relationship and letting hostility build, Tracy would end the relationship in anger without dignity. He has enough respect for Ima, now, to tell her how he feels and to end the relationship with dignity. Tracy feels sad because Ima feels hurt, but he can feel good about the way he coped with a difficult situation.

Expressing feelings to a girlfriend or boyfriend is very difficult. You are often afraid that if you tell him or her how you really feel, he or she will not like you anymore. Girls often feel that they must be agreeable and do what their boyfriend wants to do even if they would rather not. The other person in the relationship will assume that you want the same things he does unless you tell him that you do not. The other person will assume that the way you are being treated is completely acceptable to you unless you tell her that you want to be treated differently. Assertiveness gives you the method to make your feelings, wants, and needs known in a nonthreatening way.

Our society often assumes that if you are a couple, you must consider the other person's wants and needs first. You automatically put your own wants and needs in a box and concentrate outside yourself. It is important to get in touch with your true feelings and express them. It will keep you from building resentment toward your partner. As you express your feelings when coping with parents or teachers, friends or relatives, you must do the same when coping with the opposite sex. All of the ways to deal with other people are just as effective with boyfriends and girlfriends. Do not let your emotional involvement keep you from coping with assertiveness.

Coping with Peer Pressure

Young adult years are a time of wanting to be accepted by peers. That need for acceptance puts pressure on you to do things that you may not want to do. It is difficult to stand on your own and stay with your personal convictions when others are pressing you to do what they are doing. You will find yourself needing to say no to others on some occasions and to say yes to what you want at other times.

Saying no. The way to say no to peer pressure is to do just that. You need an assertive "I" statement. You only need *one*, and you use it like a broken record.

STU STONER: You wanna get high?
DEE CISIVE: No, I don't do drugs.
STU STONER: You oughta try gettin' high. It feels great!
DEE CISIVE: I don't do drugs.
STU STONER: This is killer weed. You'll really like it.
DEE CISIVE: I don't do drugs.
STU STONER: Whatsa matter, you afraid to get high?
DEE CISIVE: I don't do drugs.
STU STONER: It would probably be a waste of good stuff to give it to you anyway.

If you have quit and are trying to stay clean and not use and Stu was one of your using buddies, he will want you to get high with him and will press you.

STU STONER: Let's get high.
CONNIE VIVIAL: No, I don't do drugs.
STU STONER: Who you tryin' to kid? We got high together too many times for me to believe that.
CONNIE VIVIAL: I don't do drugs.
STU STONER: You tellin' me you quit?
CONNIE VIVIAL: That's right. I don't do drugs.

STU STONER: I got some killer weed.
CONNIE VIVIAL: I don't do drugs.
STU STONER: This stuff is soooo good.
CONNIE VIVIAL: I don't do drugs.
STU STONER: This is killer bud. You know how good that makes you feel.
CONNIE VIVIAL: I don't do drugs.
STU STONER: You gonna pass up killer bud?
CONNIE VIVIAL: I don't do drugs.
STU STONER: If that's the way you're gonna be, I'll find somebody else to get high with.

You do not have to put down the Stu Stoners. You can treat them with dignity and respect. You do not have to explain or defend your statement. Keep with it until the other person gives up. Your persistence will win for you. Some other assertive statements to use when you want to say no are: "I'm not drinking tonight." "I don't want to be sexually involved." "I don't smoke cigarettes." Whatever you are being pressured to do, you can state, "I don't. . . ." When others see that you mean what you say, they will not bother you about it anymore. You just have to hang in there a time or two.

Saying yes to yourself. When you feel that others do not agree with you, the tendency is to go along with the group. You have a right to your opinion. You are not wrong because others disagree with you. They are not wrong because you disagree with them. You disagree, that is all. You are okay, and what you think and believe are okay. Your feelings, wants, and needs are important. The Real You wants to be treated with dignity and respect. The Voice will try to talk you into being one of the gang even if it means giving up the Real You. Stay in touch with the Real You. Your self-respect demands that you say yes to your convictions. Stand up for yourself by trusting your feelings. The Real You will tell you what you are feeling. What you feel is right for you. It may not be right for others, but you are your own best judge. You are responsible for your own happiness and well-being. Pleasing others, going along with the gang, or being accepted will not bring happiness if you know within yourself that you are doing things that you really do not want to do, that you are going along with behavior that does not fit you. Say yes to yourself, and, with dignity and respect, assert your feelings, wants, and needs.

CHAPTER XI

Your Plan for Becoming Assertive

Becoming assertive is like learning to ski or learning any new skill: It takes time and practice. You cannot put on a pair of skis and expect to tackle the steep slopes. You cannot say that now that you have read about being assertive you can do everything that is explained or suggested in the book. Learning to ski means falling down. It means doing well one day and having difficulty another day. It means breaking bad habits and replacing them with new ways of thinking and moving. It means picking yourself up and realizing that you gave your feet one message and your upper body a different message. Getting body parts to work for one purpose takes concentration and practice. Progress comes bit by bit. When easy slopes are skied with ease, the intermediate slopes are tried until finally you are able to ski in control on the steeps. The bumps will give you trouble, and you will avoid some hills until you have even more skill. There is always more to learn, but you can enjoy skiing at whatever level you are on.

Learning to be assertive is the same process. You must start at an easy level and add one skill on another until you can handle more difficult situations. It will not be smooth going. Just as you must fall when you are learning to ski, you must have falls when you are learning to be assertive. You cannot change lifelong behavior patterns in one easy lesson. If you handle something inappropriately, do not worry. You will have another chance to try a more assertive way of doing it. The fact that you are uncomfortable and are aware that you could have handled things differently shows growth on your part. Give yourself credit for each step you take. Consider yourself as you would a friend and give yourself words of encouragement if you stumble or fall along the way. Allow yourself to be a beginner, and do not expect perfection. You will soon be skiing the intermediate slopes of assertiveness and then the advanced runs will be yours, too.

Steps for Becoming Assertive

Step 1. *Choose a support person.* You can become assertive by working on your own, but it will take supreme determination.

Having a support person to practice with and give you feedback will make your job easier. An adult support person is best, and a parent is ideal. Read the book together so that the adult knows what you need to do. If you cannot share with a parent, perhaps a counselor or teacher at school will work with you. You may have a neighbor, a friend's parent, an older sister or brother, or another relative you feel you can trust to help you. If you do not have an adult you feel comfortable asking to help you, work with a friend. Changing is always easier is you have someone to help you over the bumpy spots. A support person to share with is important.

Step 2. *Decide if you need to stop some destructive behavior.* In Chapter IX you were given five things to stop doing. If you are still doing those things, choose one to work on stopping this week. Work on each one for a week at a time, and add one each week until you have eliminated them from your behavior. You can go on with the other steps of your assertive plan while working on stopping these behaviors.

Step 3. *Decide to be assertive.* Being assertive is a choice. Your aggressiveness or nonassertiveness is a choice even if you have not been aware of the choice you have been making. You can choose to be assertive. It means looking at your behavior and deciding to change. When situations arise that would normally bring an aggressive reaction, you will have to stop and ask yourself how you want to handle things. It takes effort, but your payoff will be worth the effort.

To be assertive you must get in touch with your feelings and be willing to express them in "I" statements. Changing "you" messages to "I" statements takes time and effort. Remember, you are a beginner and will forget "I" and slip back to "you," but every "I" message you send is one more than you did before.

Step 4. *Determine your assertive strengths and weaknesses.* Chapter III contains an assertiveness survey. If you have not taken that survey, do it now. The areas with which you have the least trouble are the areas you can strengthen most easily. The people you feel most comfortable with are the people on whom it will be easiest for you to practice your developing assertive skills. Those areas and people that give you the most difficulty are the ones for which you will need the most support.

Step 5. *Decide where you want to start.* Always start easy. Make your first project something you know you can handle successfully. Choose the assertive area that is easiest for you. Choose at least two people to practice on, a person you feel comfortable with and a person who is difficult for you. If your area is positive assertions, practice making positive assertions to the people you have chosen. It may be easy to say positive things to your mother. Plan to say at least one positive thing to her each day for a week. Write the assertions down and practice them with your support person. Then comes the hard part. Write a positive assertion for the difficult person. It may be your Mr. Zero. He may be suspicious if you say something positive to him every day; it may be more than he (and you) can take, so do two for the week. You can continue your positive assertions beyond the week. If it feels okay, you can do positive assertions for more than one difficult person. It will be good practice for you and will help them. If your difficult person is a parent, do a positive assertion every day. You can never be too positive with parents.

After your success with positive assertions, you will be ready for the more difficult part of this step. Choose an area of assertion that is difficult for you and work on that area. Choose a person you feel comfortable with for your first try. If negative assertions are difficult for you, and you think you can handle making a negative assertion to your sister, make that your next project. Then choose a more difficult situation. You will find that once you begin, you will have many opportunities to practice assertiveness.

Step 6. *Decide if something is critical and needs immediate attention.* You may have something happening that is difficult but needs handling before it goes any further. In that case, decide how best to cope with the situation. If it is a person being very critical, what do you want to do? Refer to Chapter VIII and with your support person plan how to deal with the person. Write out your assertions and/or your strategy and practice saying them aloud. Remember how important your body language is to making an assertive presentation.

If your problem is more complicated, you may need to make a Three-Step Plan and to work very closely with your support person. Try to find a similar problem in the book to help you work out your strategy. Careful planning and preparation are important.

The outcome of your encounter may not be what you had hoped. Remember, you were trying to go down a pretty steep slope for a beginner. Give yourself credit for your efforts: You did assert yourself, and you accomplished that for yourself. Share what happened with your support person to determine what did not work, and decide what you can do differently next time. In other words, use the experience as an opportunity to learn. Do not be discouraged. You will never learn to ski if you quit just because you fall down. The most important thing a beginning skier learns is how to get up after a fall. You have to keep trying. The next run may be the one when you put it all together and go down that hill with an ease you never dreamed of.

Step 7. *Continue working on assertive behavior.* Once you get in touch with your feelings, wants, and needs and begin to take care of yourself assertively, you will find that you like the way you feel when you have coped with a situation assertively. You will be able to go to your survey and choose an area to work on or a person with whom you would like to improve your relationship and decide how you will assertively handle the situation. As things occur, you will be able to deal with them assertively. The more you cope assertively the easier it will become.

You will find that you begin to become more aware of your feelings. As that awareness becomes sharper, you will discover that you have to take care of those feelings. Often all you do is make an "I" statement of what you are feeling. It is amazing how much pressure can be relieved when you calmly say, "I feel angry." The other person does not have to do anything. The simple statement getting your feelings out in the open is all you need to take care of yourself. You may need to stomp around and huff and puff a bit and then you are okay. People sometimes say, "Don't be upset." Phooey! If you are upset, say so and ask to be allowed to be huffy for a while. "I feel angry, and I need to be mad for a few minutes. I'll be okay in a little while." It is surprising how people understand and leave you alone until you have handled your anger, providing you tell them what is happening with you.

A Final Word

The seven steps suggested here are only that—suggestions for starting your exciting assertive adventures down the ski slopes of life. You can carry your skis and hike up the hills if you want to, but you can also choose to ride the lift to the top of the hill. An adult working with you can be your lift. Your lift ticket will cost you one assertion: "I'm working on a problem, and I'd like your help." You still have to get down the hill on your own. No one can do that for you.

By taking responsibility for your feelings, wants, and needs, by owning your own problems, you take a giant step toward maturity and getting along with people. Everyone needs to be listened to and taken seriously. When you communicate with assertiveness, people listen to you. When you communicate your needs directly and honestly, people take you seriously. You will find that you no longer have to push and shove to get your needs met, nor will you have to put your wants and needs aside to keep on good terms with others. By coping with assertiveness you can maintain your rights while respecting the rights of others.

Throughout the book the theme has been that assertiveness gives you a way to treat everyone, including yourself, with dignity and respect. When you have expressed your feelings assertively, you feel that you have shown respect for the other person, and you have behaved in such a way that you respect yourself for how you dealt with the situation.

When all is said and done, you feel good about you. Feeling good about you is what assertiveness is all about.

This book offers you new patterns for putting words together, but the words and the feelings must be yours. What you say and how you say it must come from inside you, and all you need for improving your relationships with people is within you. Assertiveness can be your key for unlocking that treasure within.

Index